Lande Sport Climbs

A Climber's Guide Featuring Wild Iris, Sinks Canyon and More

Steve Bechtel

Volume 1 in the Cowboy Rock

series of climbing guides

PRESS

First Ascent Press

Livingston, MT

First Ascent Press, LLC
PO Box 2338
Livingston, MT 59047

PRESS   www.firstascentpress.com

LANDER SPORT CLIMBS
A Climber's Guide to Wild Iris, Sinks Canyon & More
by Steve Bechtel

Library of Congress Control Number: 2007925665
ISBN 10: 1-933009-063
ISBN 13: 978-1-933009-063

11   10   09   08   07   1   2   3   4   5   6   7   8   9   10

Text © 2007 Steve Bechtel
Crag Photos © Steve Bechtel
Action Photos © As Indicated. Used by permission.
Maps, Illustrations & Layout © 2007 First Ascent Press, LLC.
All Rights Reserved. Printed in the United States by McNaughton & Gunn.

Volume 1
"Cowboy Rock" Series of Wyoming Climbing Guides
Series Editor: Joe Josephson
Topos & Map Design: Moore Creative Designs – Helena, MT

Front Cover Photo: Tarris Webber climbs *Bobcat Logic* (12c) on the "Rodeo Wave" at Wild Iris. Photo © Bobby Model. www.m-11.com.

Back Cover Photo: Steve Bechtel climbing *Spurs Equal Velocity* (12a) at Wild Iris Photo © Bobby Model. www.m-11.com.

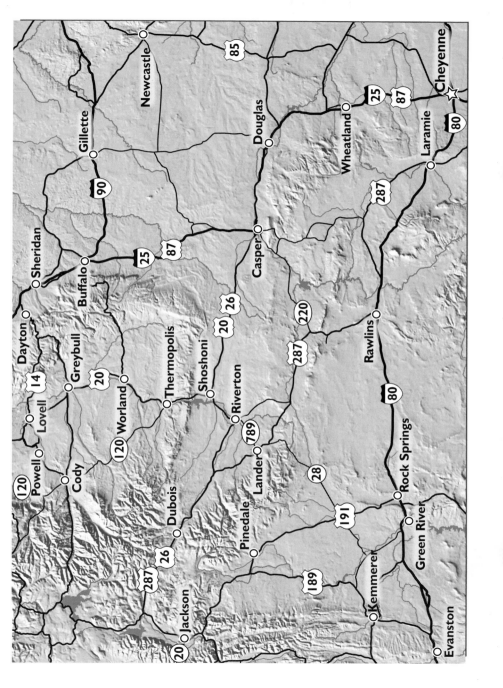

A message from BARF

We all love sport clip anchors. Many of these graced the anchors of such popular climbs as *Action Candy* and *Wind River Rose*. But the use and abuse they take from visitors and locals alike has destroyed these in a very short time.

Even the toughest stainless steel rap anchors are suffering appalling wear, and the number of climbers visiting Sinks and the Wild Iris is growing every year. Each pair of sport clips cost almost $40. If we can't slow the rate of destruction, no one will be willing or able to replace them year after year.

And so we plead: Please, please, pretty please, top rope and lower on your own gear. Sport clips, rap rings, and springers alike are there for the sole purpose of safe cleaning and aren't designed for industrial-level top roping. When you get to any anchor, clip your draws to it and lower to the ground. Only the last climber in each party should ever climb on or lower off a rope through the anchors. It only takes a few seconds to clip in a couple draws; and it saves folks time, money, and anxiety.

Established in 1993, Lander's B.A.R.F. (Bolt Anchor Replacement Fund) is funded by local individuals, the International Climbers' Festival, the Wild Iris Gumball Machine, and occasional donations from traveling climbers. If you've never put money into a new route, now's your chance to help out. Wild Iris Mountain Sports on Main Street accepts donations to BARF which helps subsidize all our anchor replacement efforts. If you enjoy the climbing here, please consider helping maintain the safety and quality of the anchors around Lander.

Wild Iris Mountain Sports
333 Main Street
Lander, WY 82520

888-284-5968 : 307-332-4541
307-335-8923 fax

www.wildirisclimbing.com
wildiris@wildirisclimbing.com

CONTENTS

Todd Skinner on *Wind Drinker*, Suicide Point.
Photo © Bobby Model. www.m-11.com

DEDICATION

This book is dedicated to my friend, Todd Skinner. Todd loved climbing more than anyone I have ever known. He was determined. He was strong. He was kind. We shall not see his like again.

"You *must* believe."

6

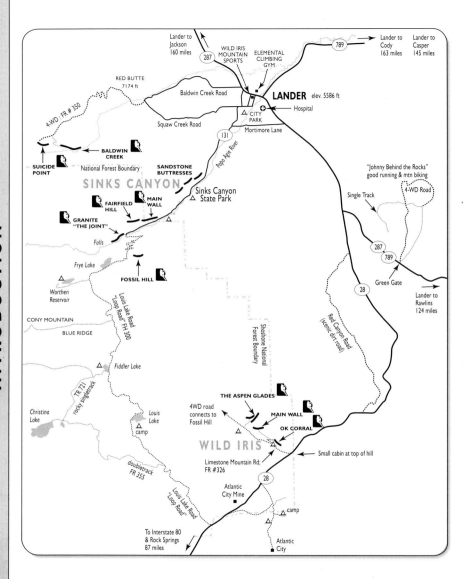

Lander to
Jackson
160 miles

Lander to
Cody
163 miles

Lander to
Casper
145 miles

287

789

WILD IRIS
MOUNTAIN
SPORTS

ELEMENTAL
CLIMBING
GYM

LANDER elev. 5586 ft

RED BUTTE
7174 ft

Baldwin Creek Road

4-WD · FR # 350

Hospital

CITY
PARK

Squaw Creek Road

Mortimore Lane

131

BALDWIN
CREEK

SUICIDE
POINT

National Forest Boundary

SANDSTONE
BUTTRESSES

Popo Agie River

SINKS CANYON

Sinks Canyon
State Park

"Johnny Behind the Rocks"
good running & mtn biking

4-WD Road

Single Track

FAIRFIELD
HILL

MAIN
WALL

GRANITE
"THE JOINT"

Falls

287

789

Frye Lake

FOSSIL HILL

Green Gate

28

Worthen
Reservoir

CONY MOUNTAIN

BLUE RIDGE

Louis Lake Road
"Loop Road" FH 300

Lander to
Rawlins
124 miles

Red Canyon Road
(scenic dirt road)

Shoshone National
Forest Boundary

Fiddler Lake

TR 721
rocky singletrack

Christina
Lake

Louis
Lake

camp

4WD road
connects to
Fossil Hill

THE ASPEN GLADES

MAIN WALL

OK CORRAL

WILD IRIS

Small cabin at top of hill

doubletrack
FR 355

Limestone Mountain Rd;
FR #326

28

Louis Lake Road
"Loop Road"

Atlantic
City Mine

camp

To Interstate 80
& Rock Springs
87 miles

Atlantic
City

🪨 : Indicates cliffs described in this edition.

Map based on original by Daniel Miller. Used by Permission.

INTRODUCTION

8

LANDER S

Welcome to Lander

Geology has been kind to climbers in Wyoming, and has been most kind near the small town of Lander, on the eastern slopes of the Wind River Mountains. For rock climbers, a day's climbing could include a trip deep into the Wind Rivers to climb alpine granite, an afternoon of limestone pocket pulling at any of fourteen developed cliffs, a little bouldering on some of the best stone in the U.S., or a day of climbing hard granite cracks in the deserts east of town.

History has also been kind to climbers here. Lander was built where it is because of the lack of wind and the rich ground of the Popo Agie (pronounced popozhia) River valley. The town existed as a small farming community for years, then a mining town, and most recently as the base of the National Outdoor Leadership School.

Lander is pretty quiet, but that works out fine if you are spending most of your time climbing. There are places to eat and sleep and buy climbing gear, and in a perfect world that would be enough.

Lander serves as a great training ground for hard rock climbing. The handful of locals you'll run into (look for the big forearms) climb here year-round and are rarely forced inside due to bad weather. Climbers from other nearby communities also use Lander as their primary rock climbing area. When the snow in the Tetons begins to melt, dozens of climbers from Jackson (look for the little forearms and big calves) make the two hour drive to the warm crags of Sinks Canyon. Climbers from Casper (big trucks), Rock Springs (big wallets), and Laramie (scars on elbows and knees), also frequent the area.

This guidebook details sport climbing on nine of Lander's best cliffs. Additional climbs on Sinks Canyon's Sandstone Buttress and Granite Buttress, the Sweetwater Rocks, and other random crags are covered in Greg Collins' *Lander Rock* (2005).

- Steve Bechtel, June 2007

INTRODUCTION

Daniel Miller climbing *Blood Brother*, Sinks Canyon.
Photo © Ken Driese. December 2004.

LANDER

ORT CLIMBS

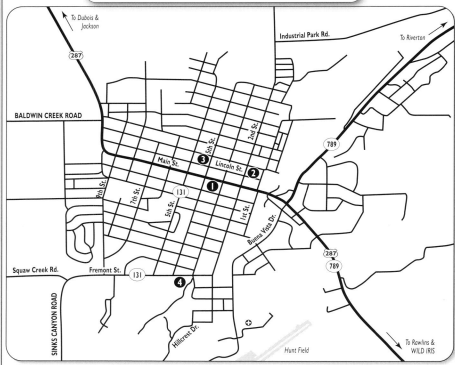

Lander, Wyoming

❶ : **WILD IRIS MOUNTAIN SPORTS** • 333 Main Street • 332-4541
❷ : **ELEMENTAL TRAINING CENTER** • 134 Lincoln Street • 332-0480
❸ : **NOLS & THE GULCH** • 502 Lincoln Street • 332-4784
❹ : **LANDER CITY PARK** • 405 Fremont Street • 332-4647

Climbing Gear and Gyms

❶ **Wild Iris Mountain Sports** is located at 333 Main Street. They have a wide range of gear and apparel. They also offer a large selection of guidebooks and maps of the Lander area and the Winds. 307-332-4541 : www.wildirisclimbing.com

❷ **Elemental Training Center** houses the local indoor climbing gym at 134 Lincoln Street. ETC offers day passes to a full fitness center and climbing gym. Showers are $5 and include use of a towel. 307-332-0480 : www.elementaltraining.com

❸ NOLS Rocky Mountain Branch and **The Gulch** are located at 502 Lincoln Street. NOLS Issue Room offers select gear and apparel while The Gulch provides a wide variety of bulk dried foods. The Gulch is a mandatory stop before heading into the Wind River Mountains. 307-332-4784 : www.nols.edu

Climbing Guides

Jackson Hole Mountain Guides (www.jhmg.com) and **Exum Mountain Guides** (www.exumguides.com), both based out of Jackson, WY, offer guiding services around Lander.

Water

❹ Water is available at the Lander City Park in the warmer months. Wild Iris Mountain Sports also has a water spigot outside their front door. Check inside before you fill up.

Brian Lenz pulling pockets on another Wild Iris classic.
Photo © Bobby Model. www.m-11.com

PORT CLIMBS

Local Food and Beverages

Lander has a number of great restaurants with many styles and ethnicities to choose from.

The Cowfish offers beef, seafood and great bowl food. *126 Main*

The Gannett Grill's patio welcomes you in the summertime to burgers and pizzas. This is THE place for climbers on the cheap. *126 Main*

The Lander Bar is Lander's most popular bar. Located right next door to the Gannett Grill. *126 Main*

El Sol de Mexico serves authentic Mexican food and effective margaritas. Take out is available. *453 Main*

Tony's Pizza has a menu full of pastas, salads and pizza. *637 W Main*

Asian Cuisine spices up Lander with a mixture of Thai, Indian and Cambodian cuisine. *140 N 7th*

The Open Door serves breakfast, lunch and coffee all day long. *159 N 2nd*

Main Street Books serves books and coffee. Open late. *300 W Main*

Chocolates for Breakfast makes delicious real fruit smoothies. A great bargain on a summer day! Located next door to Wild Iris Mountain Sports on Main Street.

Wildflour Bakery & Espresso serves bagels, sandwiches and coffee. *545 W Main*

JB's Sausage & Smokehouse offers a great selection of organic and locally grown products. *628 W Main*

China Garden serves authentic Chinese cuisine. *162 N 6th*

The Hitching Rack is a western steak house with a salad bar. Owned by the first American to climb V12. *983 Hwy 789*

The Oxbow is your classic bacon & eggs breakfast joint. *170 Main*

Safeway and **Mr. D's Grocery Store**, are both located on Main Street. Mr. D's has a bakery and deli and both have **liquor stores**.

Other restaurants

Pizza Hut, *670 E Main*
The Summit, *260 Grand View Drive*
Artic Circle, *620 W Main*
Subway, *960 W Main*
McDonalds, *235 McFarlane Drive*
Dairy Land Drive-In, *977 W Main*
Big Noi, *280 Hwy 789*
The Bread Board, *1350 Main*

LANDERS

Internet Access

The Open Door : wireless, no computers
The Fremont County Library : computers, no wireless
Wildflour Bakery : wireless, no computers

Camping, Fires & Bears

The City of Lander offers free camping in the City Park with a three day limit. There are toilets and water. See town map.

There are three campgrounds in Sinks Canyon. The first two are Forest Service fee campgrounds. They both have toilets and water. The third is a free campground with a pit toilet and no water.

Camping is also available at Wild Iris near the OK Corral. This is free camping with a 14 day limit. There is a pit toilet but no water.

Unimproved camping is also available near Baldwin Creek, Suicide Point and Fossil Hill. No services are available at these areas.

There is often a **FIRE BAN** during the summer months in and around Lander. Make sure you check before planning a campfire. Lander is also **BEAR COUNTRY** so please limit the **BLTs** in your pack and keep all camp food in hard containers inside your car.

FOSSIL HILL
elev. 9089 ft

INTRODUCTION

Greg Collins climbing *Wield the Scepter*, Sinks Canyon.
Photo © David Anderson.

LANDER

Acknowledgments

I feel great gratitude to Greg Collins, Todd Skinner, Bob Branscomb, and Paul Piana. These men have each established dozens of climbs in this area, spending many days working so that we could play. Other major sport pioneers include Frank Dusl, Ed Delong, Vance White, Heidi Badaracco, Jim Ratz, Amy Skinner, BJ Tilden, Pete Delannoy, Leif Gasch, Mike Lindsey, Tom Hargis, Sue Miller, Dave Doll, Porter Jarrard, Rick Thompson, Gary Wilmot, Rick and Jeff Leafgreen, Bobby Model, and John Hennings. Each of these people, and many others, have given valuable time to our sport and this climbing area.

Thanks especially to my wife Ellen who has made so much possible in my life, and has done so much work on this guide.

And finally thanks to Joe Josephson at First Ascent Press for morphing Lander Sport Climbs from a pile of notebooks and my crappy digital images into the book you are now holding.

INTRODUCTION

Todd Skinner, Paul Piana & "Dr. Dave" Doll, Sinks Canyon. Photo © Ken Driese. Nov 2004.

Photos Above

A fifteen year study in how "getting up a route" has evolved around Lander. Photos Courtesy Ken Driese.

Left: Ken Driese and Mark Schaeffer on the 3rd pitch of *Hawk Walk*; Sinks Canyon, Sandstone Buttress. March 1982.

Right: Steve Bechtel and BJ Tilden working an ubiquitous sport route (read: they don't remember); Sinks Canyon, Bighorn Dolomite. April 1997.

About the Author

Steve Bechtel began climbing in 1986 at Fremont Canyon, Wyoming. He likely would have quit the sport, but was not allowed to. He had been taken on as a belay slave for local legend Steve Petro in his epic quest to climb the now-legendary "Fiddler on the Roof," and quitting was not an option. In 1990, Steve was invited to climb at Sinks Canyon with his friend, Frank Dusl, who had rediscovered just how good the climbing was in his hometown. From that moment, Steve was enchanted with the wonderful climbing and the miles of beautiful, white stone in the hills outside Lander.

After finishing college at the University of Vedauwoo, Steve moved to Lander full time. Over the past twenty years, he has established over 200 new routes. These range from 25 foot sport routes to epic big wall free climbs in the greater ranges of the world. Between climbing days, he owns and operates Elemental Training Center (a climbing gym, fitness center and coaching business) with his wife, Ellen.

The Photographers

This edition would be just another ubiquitous rock climbing guide without the beautiful imagery and generosity of several additional Wyoming climbing pioneers—Bobby Model, Ken Driese and Dave Anderson. I have had the pleasure of knowing these guys for years, and feel lucky to have them as contributors to this area and to this work. The art these men create brings this area to life much more than any words I could possibly write.

For information on boulder problems around the Lander area, refer to Steve Bechtel's cleverly named *Lander Bouldering;* **available at Wild Iris Mountain Sports or on the web at www.firstascentpress.com.**

Photo Above : The Author climbing *Good Luck Mr. Gorsky* (13c).

Kirk Billings climbing *Spurs Equal Velocity*.
Photo © Bobby Model. www.m-11.com

LANDER S

SPORT CLIMBS

WILD IRIS OVERVIEW

The Limestone Mtn Road is usually inaccessible mid-November to mid-May due to snow.

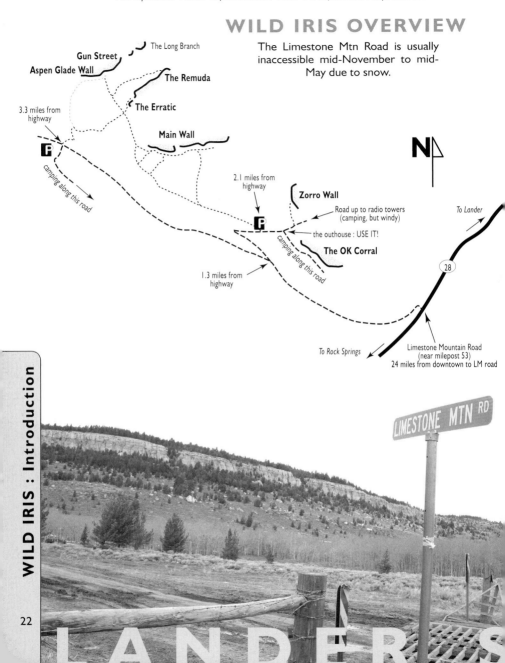

The Long Branch

Gun Street

Aspen Glade Wall

The Remuda

The Erratic

3.3 miles from highway

Main Wall

N

camping along this road

2.1 miles from highway

Zorro Wall

Road up to radio towers (camping, but windy)

To Lander

the outhouse : USE IT!

The OK Corral

camping along this road

28

1.3 miles from highway

To Rock Springs

Limestone Mountain Road (near milepost 53)
24 miles from downtown to LM road

LIMESTONE MTN RD

WILD IRIS : Introduction

22

LANDERS

WILD IRIS

The Wild Iris area is one of the most beautiful rock climbing areas in America. Bone-white stone rising on a windswept ridge has yielded some of the fiercest short climbs anywhere. This area, set on the southeast flank of the Wind River Mountains, has been a magnet for climbers seeking to push their limits for almost 20 years.

Although there had been climbers exploring this area for a few years, Todd Skinner put this area on the map when he moved to nearby Atlantic City and declared it the crag he had searched the world for. Soon after, Todd, his wife Amy, Jacob Valdez, Heidi Badaracco, Paul Piana, and a handful of others turned it into one of the most famous sport crags in the country.

Development of new routes has slowed since the early 1990s, but a few new routes get done each year. The crazy crowded days of the late 1990s are over, and Wild Iris is once again a quiet and idyllic crag most of the year. Some weekends there will only be one or two groups enjoying the now nearly 250 climbs spread across Limestone Mountain.

Wild Iris Crags

OK Corral & Zorro Wall : Page 25

Main Wall : Page 38

The Aspen Glades aka The Backside : Page 60

For this guide, I have divided the entire Wild Iris into three major areas: The OK Corral (including the OK Corral and Zorro Wall), The Main Wall (featuring everything from Rising From the Plains to the Cowboy Poetry Wall), and The Aspen Glades (which includes The Aspen Glade Wall, Gun Street, the walls of The Remuda, and The Erratic).

Some areas, such as the Longbranch, Carson City, and Lonesome Dove have not been included due to their remoteness or scarcity of established routes. For information on these climbs and others, refer to the "More Beta" page at www.firstascentpress.com.

MAP LEFT: Wild Iris Overview. Area Overview on Page 8.

See each section for specific directions.

Ellen Bechtel at Wild Iris.
Photo © Mike Lilygren.

The OK Corral is the shortest and least aesthetic dolomite cliff in the Lander area. It is also the most popular summertime crag due to the short approach and abundance of moderate routes.

The first sixteen routes described are at the Zorro section of the wall, a west facing cliff north of the main wall parking lot. These routes get afternoon sun.

The remainder of the routes are located on the cliff behind the outhouse, to the right of the large quarry. These routes face southwest, and are in the shade until about 10 a.m. in summer.

DRIVE TIME: 30 minutes from Lander

HIKE: 3 to 10 minutes flat walking

SUN EXPOSURE: A.M. shade only
Zorro, shade until Noon
OK Corral, shade until 10 a.m.

SEASON: Late Spring, Summer and Fall

LENGTH: 40 to 80 feet

OK CORRAL ROUTE COUNT by GRADE

< 5.8 : 18 — 5.9 : 5 — 5.10 : 22 — 5.11 : 23 — 5.12 : 13 — 5.13 : 3

GETTING THERE (OK Corral & Main Wall)

To reach the Wild Iris Area, drive east out of Lander on Main Street. After about 24 miles (near milepost 53), take a right on the dirt Limestone Mountain Road (this sign tends to get stolen a lot, so look for a stop sign and cattle guard, which tend to be stolen less frequently). Take this road for 1.3 miles to a fork. The left fork goes to The Aspen Glade parking area, 2.0 miles up the road. To reach parking for the Main Wall and the OK Corral, take the right fork, switchback up the hill, and park on the left as you crest the ridge (0.8 miles past the fork). The Main Wall is to the northwest, and the OK Corral behind you to the southeast.

APPROACH (Zorro Wall)

The first sixteen routes described are at the Zorro section of the wall, a west-facing cliff to the north of the Main Wall parking lot. These routes get afternoon sun. (If you are looking toward the outhouse from the main parking area, this wall is downhill to your left.) The trail can be found by walking up the main road past the outhouse about 200 feet (not the OK Corral two-track), and looking for where it splits off downhill in a group of small trees. Follow this well-worn trail about 10 minutes to the cliff, which is visible for most of the approach.

OK Corral : Zorro Wall

Routes are listed right to left as they are encountered.

1. One Trick Sheep 11b
This climb is up and right of where the trail meets the wall. 60 feet

2. Burly Binkie 12b
Just above where the trail comes to the wall, this climb is burly from the get-go. 45 feet

3. Wet Wipe-a-Whet 10b
Face and slab left of *Burly Binkie*. 45 feet

4. Huggys Pull-up 8
Easier climb on face right of *Cirque du Suave*. 40 feet

5. Cirque du Suave 10b ★
This route begins in the corner, then moves out left and up a nice prow. 70 feet

6. Gaucho 10c ★★★
A low crux leads to challenging and sustained pulling above. Great climbing! 60 feet

7. Zorro 11d ★★★
Sustained difficulty up a beautiful face. This was the first route established at Wild Iris. 75 feet

8. Poposer Cowboy 12a ★★
A less-traveled cousin to *Zorro*, but a good climb nonetheless. Ain't over 'til it's over. 75 feet

9. Salsa for the Sole 12a

Up gully left of *Poposer Cowboy*, this is the rightmost route on the high wall. 60 feet

10. El Toro 12b

Center of the high face, through bulge. Very tricky. 60 feet

11. Friend or Faux 11c ★

Leftmost of the high routes, this is the best of the three. 50 feet

12. Ewenanimity 11b ★

This climb is on the leaning block just right of the tunnel. Fun, steep, juggy. 30 feet

13. The Guns I'll Never Own 11c ★

Also on the steep block, also fun. 35 feet

14. Chapito 7

Walk through the small tunnel to a short slab on the right. This is the right of two routes with chain hangers. 40 feet

15. Chico 8

Left of *Chapito*, another embarrassment. 40 feet

16. The Hangman 10d ★

About 50 feet left of the tunnel, this is a fun route. 40 feet

ledge system

leaning pillar with tunnel behind

Trail to/from parking lot

PORT CLIMBS

> ### PARKING & APPROACH (OK Corral)
>
> The cliff is approached by any of several trails leading through the woods from the rough road that passes along in front of the cliff. Due to congestion on this road, it is recommended that climbers park at the Main Wall parking lot and walk the extra 4-6 minutes it takes to get to the majority of routes.

Tribal War Wall

1. Western Front 11d
The less-popular of two routes that climb the vertical wall with a large bulge at the top. Begins in a crack feature. 65 feet

2. Tribal War 11b ★★
Parallel to *Western Front*. A really good route with a great headwall. You'll have to work to get there, though. 65 feet

3. Stirrup Trouble 12a
Tricky, thin route on the wall facing *Tribal War*. 45 feet

4. Stone Ranger 12b ★
Good movement. A clean and pretty wall. 50 feet

5. Urban Cowboys 10c ★★
Fun climbing on good holds. 4 bolts, 40 feet

Poker-Face Alice Wall

The following routes are 25 yards east of *Urban Cowboys* and start on top of a series of big slabs. The *Poker-Face Alice* roof is hard to miss.

6. One-Eyed Jack 7 ★
Starts on big ledge system. Good climbing on short wall. 30 feet

7. Outlaws on the Run 6 ★★
On wall right of *One-Eyed Jack*, really good.

8. Poker-Face Alice 12b ★★
Climb 5.8 wall to a cold shut, then left and out roof. Obviously a little burly. 50 feet

9. Calamity Jane 13b ★
Break through the largest part of the *Poker-Face* roof. 50 feet

10. Three Charlies 7 ★
Slab route with 5 bolts. 40 feet

WILD IRIS : OK Corral

Due to the number of trees obscuring the routes it is almost impossible to get decent crag photos of the **OK Corral** cliff. In lieu of photos, use the overview topos and any relevant notes in the description to find your routes.

Routes are listed left to right as they are encountered.

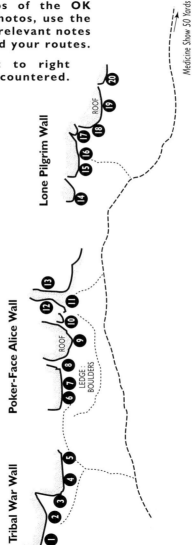

The following three routes are in a small alcove down and east of the Poker Face Alice Roof.

11. High Plains Drifter 10c ★
The left route on the left wall in a small alcove. 4 bolts, 40 feet

12. Every Gun Sings Its Own Song 11b ★
Face just right of *High Plains Drifter*. 4 bolts, 40 feet

13. Don't Bring Your Guns to Town 12c ★★
Cool black wall with crimps and big moves. 5 bolts, 45 feet

Lone Pilgrim Wall

These routes are about 100 yards east of the previous climbs. This wall is easily identified by the very clean slab of *Lone Pilgrim*.

14. Battle for a Wounded Knee 10d ★★
Starts on ledges and moves past a big bush, then up left through a concave bulge. 40 feet

15. Only the Good Die Young 11b ★
Climb seam feature to small bulge. 7 bolts, 50 feet

16. Lone Pilgrim 11d ★
Clean slab with devious moves, gets steeper high. 6 bolts, 50 feet

17. Tongue Twister 5.11b
Begin climbing crack, then move onto thin prow. 50 feet

18. Black Box 11c
Climb up slab/flake system to ledges, then up chimney/stem to a high anchor. 65 feet

19. Under the Gun 13b/c ★
Good climbing up flakes and pockets to anchor well-below huge roof (12a). Continue up slab then out 10 foot roof. 70 feet

20. Drugstore Cowboy 11c
Climb rounded arête to the right of the roof wall. 5 bolts, 40 feet

LANDER S

The Medicine Show

The next two climbs are about 75 yards from *Drugstore Cowboy*, and begin in a small alcove/chimney. They are not visible from the trail.

21. Medicine Show 7 / 12a
Easy slab starting in chimney to high hard bulge. 45 feet to first anchor, 70 feet to second.

22. Spaghetti Western 10d
Steeper route in slot facing *Medicine Show*. 5 bolts, 40 feet

Blooming Rose Wall

The following climbs are all very close together on the Red as a Blooming Rose Wall. Routes 24 to 27 face generally west. Climbs 28 to 33 face south. These climbs are located just west of where the crag trail climbs steeply to a high point before dropping back down to *Claim Jumper*.

23. Iron Horse With a Twisted Heart 9 ★
A nice slab climb on the wall west of *Red As A Blooming Rose*. 3 bolts, 35 feet

24. Give My Love To Rose 12a ★★
Hardest route on the wall. High quality pulls between small pockets. 5 bolts, 40 feet

25. Red as a Blooming Rose 10d ★★
Thin start leads to big hold climbing at the top. 5 bolts, 40 feet

26. Roll in the Hay 11a ★
Technical climbing to corner system then up ledges above. 7 bolts, 45 feet

27. Stacked Deck 10b ★★
Starts on big jugs, getting tricky higher. 5 bolts, 45 feet

28. Matilda's Last Waltz 10d
Awkward climbing up prow, left of bushy crack. 5 bolts, 45 feet

29. Cowboys are my Only Weakness 11a
Rounded prow. 4 bolts, 40 feet

30. Aces and Eights 10b ★
Starts above gnarled tree, up seams and underclings. 4 bolts, 50 feet

31. Never Sit With Your Back to the Door 10b ★★
Tricky long moves up to a small ledge. 4 bolts, 45 feet

32. Brown Dirt Cowgirl 10a ★★
Nice wall just left of corner. 3 bolts, 40 feet

33. Phat Phinger Phrenzy 8 ★
Climb up a strange corner feature. Fun. 6 bolts, 50 feet

34. Dogfight at the OK Corral 11d
Another rounded and tricky prow climb. 5 bolts, 45 feet

Claim Jumper Wall

These four climbs are just over the small hill east of *Dogfight*.

35. Claim Jumper 10c ★★★
Right-leaning lieback seam to juggy headwall. 6 bolts, 50 feet

36. Annie Get Your Drill 9 ★
Follow a crack feature on the prow then up face holds above. 6 bolts, 50 feet

37. Miner's Dee-Light 11d ★
Bouldery low moves to a nice rest then some more challenge. 5 bolts, 45 feet

38. Greenhorns in Velvet 7 ★
Very popular route up a nice clean slab. 50 feet

Winchester Wall

The three Winchester routes are on a nice long wall behind a large pine tree about 100 feet right of *Greenhorns in Velvet*.

39. Sharps 50 11a
Up slab left of *Winchester Pump*, and then up steep wall to low anchor. 50 feet

40. Winchester Pump 11a ★★
Climb center of slab, then up bulging wall on good moves. 60 feet

41. Red Ryder 10a ★★★
Follows a flake up the right slide of slab, then up nice headwall. 60 feet

LANDER S

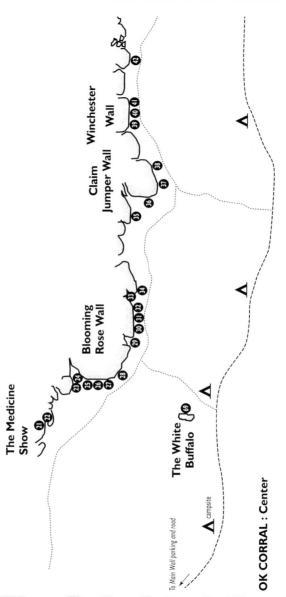

OK CORRAL : Center

Saddle Tramp Wall ─────────────────────

After *Red Ryder*, the trail meanders away from the cliff, and the routes are spaced out about 100 feet apart. The trail comes back close to the cliff at the overhanging *Saddle Tramp*.

42. Jabba the Hut 10a
Up small buttress to high long chain anchor. 50 feet

43. 30 Seconds on Fremont Street 11b ★
Bouldery climbing up short clean wall. 35 feet

44. Back in the Saddle 10c
Somewhat tricky route up west-facing wall. 40 feet

45. The Saddle Tramp 12a ★
Up bulge on undercuts and thin pockets. 40 feet

46. Whips, Chaps, and Chains 11d ★★
Rightward trending route up pockets and edges through bulge. 40 feet

Diamond Wall ──────────────────────

47. Boob Loob 10a ★
Climbs rounded bear-hug prow and high up wall above. 65 feet

48. Diamonds and Rain 11d ★★
Clean, vertical white face with cold shut anchors. 4 bolts, 45 feet

49. Scary Canary 8
Runout face climbing right of crack. A lame attempt at "bold" climbing. 50 feet

50. When the Man Comes Around 12c ★★
Bouldery short face with four bolts. 35 feet

51. Bull of the West 8
Short route with four bolts to anchor below small tree. 40 feet

52. Guns of Diablo 8
Adjacent short route. 40 feet

OK CORRAL : Right Side

La Vaca Wall ────────────────────────────

53. Sugarfoot 10c
Powerful little route that starts behind a big flake.

54. Slave 8
Face behind flake. 35 feet

55. "R" is for Redneck 7
Slab climb that starts just right of flake, and left of a big crack. 35 feet

56. La Vaca Peligrosa 8 ★★
Nice climb right of large crack. 40 feet

Pronghorn Pinnacle ────────────────────

The following three climbs are on a nice wall behind a group of large trees. These are just west of the obvious tiny "Pronghorn Pinnacle". Two more routes are found on the pinnacle itself.

57. Britchen Strap 9
Nice route with thin start. 45 feet

58. Licorice Stick 8 ★
Again, a hard start to easier rock above. 45 feet

59. Saddle Up 9 ★
Hardest of the three. 45 feet

60. Pronghorn Pinnacle 8
The west face of the small "Pronghorn Pinnacle" that sits in front of the cliff. 3 bolts. 20 feet

61. Nouveau Western 10a
This climb takes an arête on the east side of the pinnacle. 25 feet

WILD IRIS : OK Corral

LANDER S

Rodeo Drive

These routes are on the nice walls past the pinnacle. This quiet area is worth a visit.

62. The Hanging Tree 9 ★

Slab climb 50 feet right of *Pronghorn Pinnacle*, behind a few large pines. 45 feet

63. Ticks for Chicks 8 ★★

Dark slab left of chimney feature, faces southeast. 4 bolts, 40 feet

64. Route 64 10d

Face just right of prow and left of junk rock. 4 bolts, 40 feet

65. The Man From Laramie 10c ★

This route climbs a rounded prow feature past several horizontals, ending at anchors below a blocky bulge. 55 feet

66. Rodeo Drive 11c

Climb grey slab 15 feet right of rounded white prows. 4bolts, 40 feet

67. The Solace of Bolted Faces 12a ★★

Climb slab with seams just left of a crack with big bushes in it. 45 feet

68. Drinking Dry Clouds 12c ★

A four bolt route up a pretty little bulge at the very right end of the cliff band. 35 feet

The White Buffalo

69. The White Buffalo V11 or 13d ★

This is a short and savage route on a beautiful clean boulder near the third campsite on the left. It is on an east-facing wall and is visible from the camp road.

For more bouldering in the Lander area, refer to Steve Bechtel's cleverly named *Lander Bouldering;* **available at Wild Iris Mountain Sports or at www.firstascentpress.com.**

LANDER S

This is the crag that started it all. It's not the first crag that was developed in the area, nor does it have the greatest number of routes, but it's the one that put Lander on the map. The routes are short and powerful affairs and the perfect white stone is magic to climb on. Each section of this cliff has its own distinct character; from the beautifully steep Rodeo Wave, to the "thug" bulges of the Hot Tamale, to the clean verticality of Cowboy Poetry.

Expect warm days in the summer, and perfect cool conditions all fall. Take care in hiking the ridge back to the parking lot during afternoon thunderstorms. This hike is very exposed to the elements. It's best to just wait out these short storms and hike out a few minutes later than you'd planned.

DRIVE TIME: 30 minutes from Lander

HIKE: 20 to 25 minutes flat

SUN EXPOSURE: Sunny from dawn until 7 p.m.

SEASON: Late Spring, Summer and Fall

LENGTH: 25 to 80 feet

WILD IRIS : Main Wall

MAIN WALL ROUTE COUNT by GRADE

<5.9 : 5 — 5.10 : 26 — 5.11 : 21 — 5.12 : 25 — 5.13 : 10. — 5.14 : 4

Steve Bechtel climbing *Bobcat Logic* **(12c).**
Photo © Bobby Model. www.m-11.com

SPORT CLIMBS

GETTING THERE (Main Wall & OK Corral)

To reach the Wild Iris Area, drive east out of Lander on Main Street. After about 24 miles (near milepost 53), take a right on the dirt Limestone Mountain Road (this sign tends to get stolen a lot, so look for a stop sign and cattle guard, which tend to be stolen less frequently). Take this road for 1.3 miles to a fork. The left fork goes to The Aspen Glade parking area, 2.0 miles up the road. To reach parking for the Main Wall and the OK Corral, take the right fork, switchback up the hill, and park on the left as you crest the ridge (0.8 miles past the fork). The Main Wall is to the northwest, and is clearly visible from the parking lot.

WILD IRIS : Main Wall

LANDER

Routes are listed left to right as they are encountered.

WILD IRIS : Main Wall

PORT CLIMBS

Bill Hickok

Raising from the Plains

1. Rising From The Plains 12b ★★

This is the leftmost (west) route on the Wild Iris Main Wall. Climb a vertical white wall to a grey streak that goes through a short bulge. 40 feet

2. Cowboy Killer 12d ★★

Follow a zigzag bolt line up through the right side of the bulge. 40 feet

3. Project.

Anchors only. Up slab to flake. 40 feet

4. A Slug of the Old What-For 13d ★

This long-standing project was finally sent literally within hours of this edition going to printer. Begin up *Adi-Goddang-Yos*, then track left across the belly of the big bulge. 35 feet

5. Adi-Goddang-Yos 13b?

Begin in a right-facing corner, then up and right through a very steep bulge to a baffling crux. Possibly harder due to broken hold? 40 feet

6. You Ain't Bill Hickok 14a ★

Straight out the big belly. 45 feet

7. Last Man Standing 13b ★★

Climb up steep belly (using first bolt of *Hickok*) to nice climbing on overhanging wall. 45 feet

--- **Chaps Wall**

8. Pocket Derringer 11a

Harder start through low bulge leads to long moves up slab. 50 feet

9. Crazy Hörst 12b

Six feet right of *Pocket Derringer*, follow a grey streak past five bolts. 50 feet

10. Project. High bolt only.

11. The Lord Loves a Hangin' 13a

Behind a big tree, climb up a seam feature past six bolts to a cold shut anchor. 50 feet

12. Chaps 12d

Follows a black streak past four bolts. 45 feet

13. Horsewhipped and Hogtied 12d ★★

Climb left and up seam to very crimpy crux. 6 bolts, 50 feet

14. Très Hombres 13a

Slightly overhanging on slightly terrible holds. Anchor near a small pine. 5 bolts, 40 feet

Rodeo Wave Wall ──────────────────────

15. The Ranch 12d

Steep line tucked between slab and wave. 35 feet

16. Bobcat Logic 12c ★★★

Climb up big holds on the leftmost line off the slab. Most climbers clip the first bolt of *Cow Reggae* to keep the rope out of the way. 35 feet. See Cover Photograph.

17. Cow Reggae 13b ★★

A popular and fun route, the straight up line just right of *Bobcat Logic*. 4 bolts, 35 feet

WILD IRIS : Main Wall

LANDERS

18. Babalouie 12c ★★

Takes the first two bolts of *Cow Reggae*, then moves right to finish the final two of *Atomic Stetson*. 4 bolts, 35 feet

19. Atomic Stetson 13c ★★

This is the third straight up line from the left. 40 feet

20. Atomic Cow 13d ★★

Starts as *Atomic Stetson*, then traverses left onto *Cow Reggae* where *Babalouie* goes right. Slightly harder than *Atomic Stetson*. 45 feet

21. Rodeo Free Europe 14a ★★

This route goes up the longest part of the wave. The hardest of the straight up lines. 50 feet

22. Genetic Drifter 14b

Starts on *Rodeo Free Europe*, drifts left on *Atomic Stetson*, then finishes *Cow Reggae*. 55 feet

23. Rodeo Active 14a? ★

The right-most line. A very hard move (now even harder since a hold broke) leads to relatively easy climbing above. 45 feet

Wild Horses Wall

24. Project. NFR

Longstanding project.

25. Two Kinds of Justice 12b ★★

Begins behind a large blocky formation. Popular, with long and bouldery moves all the way. 40 feet

26. Gored By Inosine 12d ★

A pretty wall with very long moves. Look for a big hueco to identify this climb. 40 feet

27. Limestone Cowboy 12a ★

Behind the big pine; start with a small overhang; climb up nice rock. 45 feet

28. Hip Boot Romance 10d

A little bit strange, but a decent climb. 45 feet

29. Pronghorn Love 11d

Awkward moves lead up a pretty wall. 50 feet

30. The Prospect 10d ★★

Starts in left-facing corner, then up big pockets. 50 feet

31. The Devil Wears Spurs 10d ★★

Famous and popular, this route is getting slick! Start with big pockets near "double" pine tree. 50 feet

32. Posse On My Tail 11d ★

Bouldery climbing leads to a tricky wall above. 50 feet

33. Wild Horses 11b

Start near small corner/chimney, then up lower angled wall above. 50 feet

34. Jackalope and Boomslang 10a

Climbs the low-angle wall right of the main Wild Horses Wall. 45 feet

SPORT CLIMBS

Zen Boulden climbing *Two Kinds of Justice* **(12b).**
Photo © Ken Driese. 1999.

LANDERS

35. In God's Country 12b

Up wall through small bulges and awkward sequences. A little sharp, but takes a pretty line. This is the leftmost route on the Hot Tamale Wall. 45 feet

36. Ruby Shooter 12b ★★

Popular route with great movement. 55 feet

37. Hot Tamale Baby 11d ★★★

Also popular, with great movement. Begin in a little left-facing corner leading to rounded prow. Wanders a bit at top. 60 feet

38. Hey, Mr. Vaquero 12c ★★

Follows a grey streak. Breaks through the left side of the low bulge on long moves, then up a tricky headwall. 70 feet

39. Mexican Rodeo 12d ★★

The hardest of the bulges followed by the hardest headwall. There is a large pocket right at first bolt. 70 feet

40. Charro 12b ★★★

Big moves on big holds, then up tricky slab and past small roof. Look for underclings to identify the start. 75 feet

41. Caballero Del Norté 11d ★

Fun hard start to thin moves high. 50 feet

42. Windy City 9 ★★

Follow a corner/crack system, then climb right to anchors at the top. 50 feet

43. Popo Agie Pocket Pool 10a ★

This route is left of a big dead tree right next to the wall. Good climbing up to share anchors with *Windy City*. 50 feet

WILD IRIS : Main Wall

WILD IRIS : Main Wall

44. Osita 11a ★★
Hard move low to easier slab above. Just right of dead tree. 5 bolts, 45 feet

45. Digital Stimulation 10c
Big pockets into tricky seam. Faces east and starts off small ledge. 4 bolts, 40 feet

46. The Shootist 10a ★
Good pockets up clean wall. 5 bolts, 40 feet

47. Wind River Rose 9 ★★
Nice slab climbing up rounded prow. 5 bolts, 45 feet

48. Ryobi Jr. 10b ★

Starts on ledge system left of the Five Ten Wall. Face left of tree. 4 bolts, 40 feet

49. Ryobi Rustler 10d

From ledge system, climb right of tree up orange streak. 5 bolts, 40 feet

50. Ryobi Wrangler 11a ★

Climb off right side of ledge system, up black streak. 4 bolts, 40 feet

51. Ryobi Ranger 10a ★★

The leftmost route on the Five Ten Wall itself. Climbs up to big pockets, then through some reachy moves before easing up at the top. 5 bolts, 50 feet

52. Indian Country 10b ★★

Most climbers start on the small ledge to the right, then move up and left to good pockets. 4 bolts, 50 feet

53. Dynamitic 7 ★

Up left-facing corner about 10 feet left of the large "Stonehenge" rock that sits in front of the wall. 5 bolts, 45 feet

54. Sacagawea 10b

Starts behind left side of "Stonehenge" rock. Thin hard moves. 3 bolts, 45 feet

55. Pistol Pete 10d

Starts behind right side of "Stonehenge" rock. Thin hard moves. 4 bolts, 45 feet

56. Wild Horses Keep Dragging Me Away 10c ★

Another hard slabby face. 5 bolts, 45 feet

57. You Picked a Fine Climb to Lead Me, Lucille 9 ★

Surprisingly long moves up a streak lead to easier climbing above. Ends near a small pine tree. 40 feet

58. Latex Cowboy 10b ★★

Ten feet left of bushy crack. Steeper climbing on good pockets. (no photo) 5 bolts, 40 feet

59. T & T 10c ★

Clean white wall 15 feet left of chockstone chimney. (no photo) 5 bolts, 40 feet

Five Ten Wall
100 feet

60. Pistols and Gri Gris 11a

These routes are 50 to 60 feet right of the main Five Ten Wall. Hard moves low to lower-angle wall above. 4 bolts, 45 feet

61. War Paint 11b

Very bouldery low moves, to easier climbing above. Shares anchors with *Pistols and Gri Gris*. 4 bolts, 45 feet

62. "Dances With Wolves" & "Wind in His Hair" 7 TR

Up the gully right of *War Paint*. 20 foot clean wall.

PORT CLIMBS

Dave Body climbing *Wind & Rattlesnakes* **(12a).**
Photo © Bobby Model. www.m-11.com

LANDER S

Rode Hard Wall

63. Project. Jones on the Jukebox
This project takes the unlikely line out the bottom of a huge block leaning against the left end of the *Rode Hard* roof.

64. Copenhagen Angel 13b ★
Up white wall to climb through the biggest part of the roof. Face up to roof is 5.11. 7 bolts, 60 feet

65. Phony Express 12b ★
Starts same as *Rode Hard*, moves left on good pockets through roof. 7 bolts, 60 feet

66. Rode Hard and Put Up Wet 12c ★★
Climb clean slab starting on left side of flake/crack, heading toward "hueco" in the roof. Devious sequence through center of roof. This was the first route at the Main Wall. 6 bolts, 55 feet

67. Nine Horse Johnson 11c ★★
Up flake to vertical wall with good pockets. Out roof on jugs and stems. 6 bolts, 55 feet

68. Wind and Rattlesnakes 12a ★★★
Up nice prow, great continuous climbing. 5 bolts, 50 feet

69. Tomahawk Slam 12a ★
Crack/jug climbing to stinger move, then easier to top. 6 bolts, 50 feet

70. Easy Ridin' 10d ★★★
Great climbing up flakes to small bulge and up fun wall. 8 bolts, 55 feet

71. Arizona Cowgirl 11c ★★
Thin moves to easier wall above. This is the leftmost climb on the *Buckskin Billy* Slab. 7 bolts, 50 feet

72. Cowboy Joe 10c ★
A bulge low leads to easier climbing high. 50 feet

73. Buckskin Billy 10a ★
Tricky through the bulge, then great moves up to anchor. 45 feet

74. Hired Guns 11d
Around right of the *Buckskin Billy* slab, this route is a thin and tricky pursuit. 4 bolts, 40 feet

75. Gumby 11a

Fifteen feet left of *Latex*. Climb slab then bulge.

76. The Devil Wears Latex 10c ★★

This short route is left of the main Cowboy Poetry Wall, good pockets and fun moves. 5 bolts, 45 feet

77. Even Cowgirls Get The Blues 11a

Up bulgy wall, sneaks through bulges on right side. 60 feet

78. Testosterone Alfresco 10d ★

Shares the start of *Sleeping Thunder*, moving left after 25 feet. Up prow and over a small bulge. 55 feet

79. Sleeping Thunder 12a ★

Good climbing up vertical wall to a crux high, usually marked by a bail biner. 65 feet

80. Cowboy Poetry 11b/12a ★★★

P1 Up slab to scoop, then tricky long moves to anchor at horizontal (11b). 7 bolts, 50 feet

P2 From horizontal clip bolt up and right, then fight through bulges to upper anchor. 3 bolts, 30 feet

81. Cowboy Gibberish 11b

Left variation finish of *Cowboy Poetry*. Easier climbing into corner above. 65 feet

82. Take Your Hat Off 10b ★★★

Hard start to jug climbing, ending at anchor below bulge. 6 bolts, 50 feet

83. Boy 13a ★

Continue up headwall above *Take Your Hat Off*. 4 bolts, 35 feet

84. Buffalo Soldier 10b ★

Edgy climbing starting on flake. 5 bolts, 45 feet

85. Charlie Drew That Spinnin' Bull 12c ★

Continues through bulges above *Buffalo Soldier*.

Lauren Edwards climbing *Tomahawk Slam* **(12a).**
Photo Opposite © David Anderson.

WILD IRIS : Main Wall

86. Cowboys Don't Shoot Straight 10c ★

Up black streak below the obvious cracks in the upper bulge. 5 bolts, 50 feet

87. Pokey 5.11a

Climb the crack system above *Cowboys Don't Shoot Straight*. 65 feet

88. Ambush in the Night 11a ★

Tricky thin moves just left of small pine against the wall. 5 bolts, 45 feet

89. Riata Man 12c ★

Up bulging wall with obvious big pockets above *Ambush in the Night*. 4 bolts, 40 feet

90. Princess and the Playmate 10c ★★

First route right of small pine, low bulge to slab. 6 bolts, 50 feet

WILD IRIS : Main Wall

91. Cherokee With a Crewcut 11a ★
Climb up seam and through steep wall above with black streak.
5 bolts, 50 feet

92. Slapping Leather 11c
Start in seam then to right and steeper terrain. 5 bolts, 60 feet

93. Concrete Cowboys 10c
Wanders up and left, then back right to anchor. 5 bolts, 45 feet

94. Honed on the Range 11c ★★
Tricky route behind large pine tree. 6 bolts, 50 feet

95. Hand-Tooled Saddle 11c
On wall 100 feet right of *Honed*, up seams in steep wall.

96. Bucky Goldstein 12b
Thin face.

Cowboy Poetry Wall

WILD IRIS : Main Wall

95 96

PORT CLIMBS

Dave Body climbing *Bronc Twister* (13a).
Photo © Bobby Model. www.m-11.com

WILD IRIS : The Aspen Glades

The Aspen Glades (aka The Backside) area of Wild Iris is home to some of the best climbs anywhere. The valley behind the Main Wall includes the cliffs of The Aspen Glade, Remuda, and The Erratic. The Aspen Glade Wall features some of the cleanest stone at Wild Iris. This wall faces southeast and is pleasant late into the fall. For summer climbing, the walls of The Remuda and Erratic offer shade most of the day. Be warned, though, that the routes on these walls tend to be very difficult – this is not a beginner's crag. Also in this little valley are the crags known as The Longbranch and Lonesome Dove. Because of their remoteness and lack of route density, they will not be covered in this edition.

DRIVE TIME: 35 minutes from Lander

HIKE: 30 to 40 minutes up and down hills

SUN EXPOSURE: Aspen Glade – sunny until 4 p.m. most of the year
Remuda & Erratic – shade most of the day

SEASON: Late Spring, Summer and Fall

LENGTH: 40 to 90 feet

ASPEN GLADES ROUTE COUNT by GRADE

5.10 : 10 — **5.11** : 24 — **5.12** : 12 — **5.13** : 4 — **5.14** : 2

GETTING THERE & PARKING (The Aspen Glades)

To reach The Aspen Glades, drive east out of town on Main Street. After about 25 miles, take a right on the dirt Limestone Mountain Road (this sign tends to get stolen a lot, so look for a stop sign and cattle guard, which tend to be stolen less frequently). Take this road for 1.3 miles to a fork. The Main Wall parking and the OK corral are up the right fork. To get to The Aspen Glades, stay left at the fork. Take this road about 2 miles until you begin to enter a wooded area. Look for parking on the left, near a less-traveled dirt road. From this parking area, walk back up Limestone Mountain Road about 50 yards, and take a trail through the woods to the left (north).

PORT CLIMBS

APPROACH (The Aspen Glades aka The Backside)

The hike takes you out of the woods and switchbacks to the crest of the ridge. From here, you can see the cliffs. Walk roughly east on a trail that is occasionally a two track, following cairns. The trail drops down into a little valley and eventually to a 4-way intersection near some large dead trees. To reach the Aspen Glade, go left at this intersection. This should be really obvious, as there is a big cliff to your left with an aspen glade in front of it. To reach The Remuda, also go left, but bear right before reaching The Aspen Glade wall (see map below). The Erratic is reached by going straight at the intersection. You really can't miss it. Going right leads you uphill and to the very west end (Rising From the Plains) of the Main Wall.

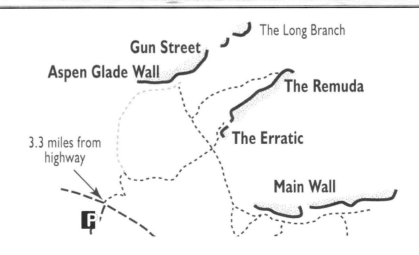

The Long Branch

Gun Street

Aspen Glade Wall

The Remuda

3.3 miles from highway

The Erratic

Main Wall

Gun Street Area

9   10   11   18   26

Routes are listed left to right

The Climbs

Climbs on The Aspen Glade Wall are described left to right. This wall can be approached via a trail that comes in along the cliff from the west to route #1, or by following the trail in from the 4-way intersection at the dead trees. If this approach is used, you reach the cliff at route #16.

1. Ambuscado 11d ★★

Follows very steep line on back of huge, leaning detached slab. 100 feet left of *Spurs* wall. 4 bolts, 35 feet

2. Night-Flying Woman 10d ★★

Starts right of bushy gully, then up great rock on good holds. 5 bolts, 40 feet

3. Buffalo Skull 11d ★

Good climbing. Used to be weird at top, but new anchor placement is better. 8 bolts, 70 feet

4. Straight Outta Hudson 12c ★★

Bouldery through roof at bottom, up slab, then through biggest part of upper roof. 9 bolts, 70 feet

5. Spurs Equal Velocity 12a ★★

Climb through right side of low roof (5.11), then up slab to six foot roof. 70 feet

6. Mutt Ridin' Monkey 10d

A bit sharp, but pretty fun climbing. 60 feet

7. Californios 11c

Starts just left of small corner, up steep face to share anchors with *Mutt Ridin' Monkey*. 60 feet

8. Hillbilly Hoedown 12a

On large block downhill and right of *Spur Equal Velocity* wall. See photo page 62. Steep face with wandering bolts. 40 feet

9. Prime Bovine Arête 11c

On the buttress halfway between *Spurs* and *Gun Street*, up a hourglass prow. See photo page 63. 5 bolts, 50 feet

10. Lonesome Cowboy 10c ★

Good climbing, but really short. See photo page 63. 3 bolts, 30 feet

WILD IRIS : Aspen Glades

LANDERS

11. Miss Yvonne Rode the Horse 11b ★

Four bolts to clip anchors. See photo page 63. 30 feet

12. Little Buckaroo 11b ★★★

Really fun. Three bolts to clip anchors. On west-facing wall. 25 feet

13. Bovine Intervention 10d ★

Just right of *Little Buckaroo* pillar, long moves up vertical wall to short crux. 6 bolts, 50 feet

14. Lonely are the Brave 11a ★★

Up steep wall with good holds to crux finish. 5 bolts, 45 feet

15. Don't Paint Your Wagon 12a ★★

Good pockets and good moves. Tricky. 5 bolts, 45 feet

16. Branded 12a

Up center of wall, follows flakes and small pockets. 5 bolts, 45 feet

17. Butch Pocket and the Sundance Pump 11d ★★★

Nice moves on big holds up seam feature to an attention-getting crux. 6 bolts, 50 feet

18. Gun Street Girl 12b ★★★
Good climbing up sinker pockets to high crux. 7 bolts, 50 feet

19. Sweet Tart of the Rodeo 10d
Powerful moves up short overhanging face to lower angle top. 7 bolts, 45 feet

20. Dirt Bag 11d ★
Begins atop orange-lichened flake. Ascend though bulges, trending left. Strange position, but good moves. 8 bolts, 50 feet

21. Sweating Bullets 10a
Up left side of slabby wall. 5 bolts, 45 feet

22. Sweaty Bully 10b ★★
Good climbing up steep rock to slab. 6 bolts, 50 feet

23. Whiskey Toast 11d
Hard long moves. A bit sporty toward the top. 5 bolts, 50 feet

24. Fist Full of Quickdraws 11d ★★
Good moves on nice rock. 6 bolts to chain anchor. 50 feet

25. The Quick and the Dead 11d ★
Tricky climbing on sloping pockets. Good route. 6 bolts, 50 feet

26. Bronc Twister 13a ★★
Up dancy slab to two-tiered roof. 5.12+ though first roof, move left, then the business. 9 bolts, 75 feet

27. Cowboy King 13b/c ★★★
Shares start with *Bronc Twister*. After first roof crux, breaks right where BT breaks left. 9 bolts, 75 feet

28. American Beauty 12b ★★★
Hard move low, then up to long roof moves. 9 bolts, 75 feet

29. Jolly Rancher 12c ★
Very tricky low face to easier climbing at top. 70 feet

30. Choke Cherry Eyes 12a ★★
Continuous fun moves up vertical wall then through bulge at top. 70 feet

WILD IRIS : Aspen Glades

LANDERS

Paul Piana climbing *Cowboy King* (13b/c).
Photo © Bobby Model. www.m-11.com

The Erratic

This cliff is actually a huge tilted boulder. It has the highest concentration of hard moves in the area, and is an absolutely beautiful piece of stone. One of the first and best 5.14s in America, *Throwin' the Houlihan* has had many ascents and is considered a gold-standard 14a.

To help orient yourself to The Erratic and The Remuda, see Aspen Glades Map on Page 62.

APPROACH (The Erratic)

Routes are described right to left, as they are encountered along the trail. Routes 1-5 are on the Erratic itself, routes 6-11 are another 150 yards downhill and east on a nice buttress.

67

PORT CLIMBS

1. Throwin' the Houlihan 14a ★★★

Step off boulder then up long moves on small pockets. The direct start boulder problem has been climbed, raising the route difficulty slightly. 50 feet

2. Project. Moonshine

Up prow/seam to very unlikely moves. 50 feet

3. Ghost Moon 13d

Starts first two bolts of *Moonshine*, then left to finish on *Heart Full of Ghosts*. 50 feet

4. Heart Full of Ghosts 14a ★★

Takes the line just left of a prow on monos and long moves. 50 feet

5. When I Was a Young Girl, I Had Me a Cowboy 13a ★★

Up steep left side of the *Erratic* with many possible sequences. 45 feet

6. Wutang 11b

Just right of *Wotai*, has a slab crux low. Tricky. 45 feet

7. Wotai 10d ★★★

Start in crack, then move right onto nice face with a small roof at the anchors. 45 feet

LANDERS

8. Whoa Nelly 5.11b ★

This climb is around left of *Wotai*, facing east. Up flakes and thin moves left of prow. 45 feet

9. Big Medicine 10b

Grey slab with thin moves, faces west. 55 feet

10. Pale Face Magic 10d

Climb up right facing corner then out right and up tricky, sharp face above. 55 feet

11. Medicine Man 11c ★★

Down around corner from *Pale Face Magic*, climb up dihedral, then out bulging wall to right. 50 feet

The following five routes are on the wall downhill and east of *Medicine Man*. **150 to 200 yards of bushwhacking will get you there.**

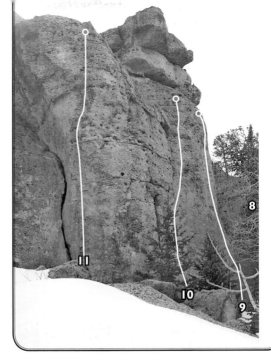

12. The Ugly 11c

Face left of seam through small bulge. 40 feet

13. The Bad 11b

Clean face with thin pockets, moving left at top. 40 feet

14. The Good 11c

Prow/face to steeper rock above. 40 feet

15. Angel Eyes 5.11b

Climb prow between obvious cracks left of *The Good*. 4 bolts, sling anchor, 40 feet

16. Tuco 5.11a

About 50 yards left of *Angel Eyes* (no photo). Not recommended. 50 feet

The Remuda

A remuda is a herd of horses from which cowboys will choose their mounts for the day. The Remuda here is a small but shady crag where climbers can escape the sun on the hottest of summer days.

Routes are described right to left as they are encountered.

APPROACH (The Remuda)

The Remuda is best reached by heading north (downhill toward the Aspen Glade Wall) from the 4-way intersection at the dead trees. Keep right where the path splits, heading downhill into the trees keeping right of the drainage. Follow this trail for 10 to12 minutes (further than you think you should go...) until it reaches the beautiful clean walls that make up The Remuda. The trail reaches the wall near *Court n' Spark*.

---

17. Court n' Spark 12b ★★★

Good moves through thin face, then up nice prow. Ends on ledge. 55 feet

18. Buck a Move 13a

That's one small pocket! One short crux to much easier climbing above. 45 feet

19. The Devil's Herd 12a ★

Shares start with *Ghost Rider*, then moves right at upper bulge. 55 feet

20. Ghost Rider 11d ★

Up prow. Crux at bottom and at top. Popular but not classic. 55 feet

21. Pedophile Moustache 11c

Starts right of *Crooked Darlin'*, but climbs straight up, crossing that route and ending slightly left. 5B 40 feet

22. Crooked Darlin' 11a

Diagonal line. A bit contrived, but easier than other route on the wall. 7 bolts, 45 feet

The following three routes are on the clean wall 100 feet left of *Crooked Darlin'*.

23. Burnt Beans and Coffee 12c ★★★

Long pulls between big pockets, with a tough crux at the end. (no photo) 6 bolts, 60 feet

24. Silverbelly 12d ★★★

Up center of beautiful white wall, long moves on little pockets. (no photo) 6 bolts, 55 feet

25. Coyote Vacuum 12b ★★

On the very left side of the *Silverbelly* wall, start in underclings, then tricky moves to the top. (no photo) 5 bolts, 40 feet

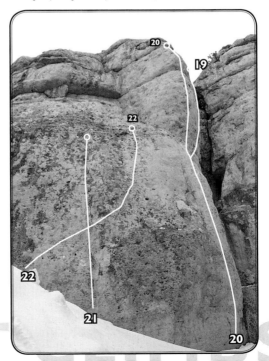

LANDERS

SINKS CANYON

Sinks Canyon is the centerpiece of Lander climbing. Located just seven miles from downtown, this area features climbing on dozens of different cliffs consisting of three very different rock types. In a mere four miles, this unique canyon cuts through sandstone, dolomite and granite. For the purposes of this edition, we will cover only the major sport climbing cliffs on the sunny side of the canyon. Two of these (the Sinks Main Wall and Fairfield Hill Wall) are bighorn dolomite, featuring long, steep pocketed routes. The third, The Joint, is a short and slick granite cliff that sits near the head of Sinks Canyon.

Major development of the sport climbing cliffs began years after climbers discovered the other walls of Sinks. As early as the 1960s the sandstone walls low in the canyon were a playground for mountaineers practicing their skills for the higher peaks of the Wind River Range. Many of these routes remain popular for those interested in more adventerous trad climbing. It wasn't until the late 1980s, though, that the dolomite cliffs drew much attention. The period from about 1990 to 2000 saw massive development of the dolomite and, with over 320 climbing days a year, has seen a large influx of climbers from all over the world.

There are now over 400 sport routes in the canyon. Add this to the myriad routes on the sandstone and granite buttresses, and you've got a destination area for all types of rock climbers.

The Sinks Canyon Road is open year round and in winter the Main Wall is the warmest and most sheltered from the wind.

Sinks Canyon Crags

The Shady Side : Not covered in this edition

Sandstone Buttresses : Not covered in this edition

Bighorn Dolomite, Main Wall : Begins on page 75

Bighorn Dolomite, Fairfield Hill : Begins on page 121

Granite Buttresses, The Joint : Begins on page 133

For overview of Sinks Canyon, see Area Map on page 8.

Georgie Stanley climbs *Brown Trout* **(11c)**
Photo Opposite © Bobby Model. www.m-11.com

GETTING THERE (Sinks Canyon)

From Main Street in Lander, turn south on either 5th or 9th Street and go for less than a mile to where it T-bones with the "Sinks Canyon Road," Highway 131. Turn right. Just out of town, stay left where the Sinks Road forks with Squaw Creek Road. Continue almost 6 miles to the obvious entrance sign for the "Sinks Canyon State Park."

Sawmill Picnic Area is another 1/4 mile followed in the next mile and half or so by the State Park Visitor Center (limited hours) and then the Popo Agie Campground. All three of these facilities have restrooms and it is highly encouraged to use them before heading to the crags.

3/4 of a mile past the Popo Agie Campground is a cattleguard indicating the switch from State Park to Forest Service land. All of the routes listed here are approached up canyon from here. See specific parking and approach details under the sections for the Main Wall, Fairfield Hill and The Joint.

Tom Kalakay in Sinks Canyon
Photo © Ken Driese

LANDER

SINKS CANYON : Main Wall

The Main Wall of Sinks is, arguably, the most consistently climbable crag in the country; this wall is good both in mid-winter and mid-summer. As the sun rises higher in the sky during the summer months, the crag tends to get more shade, in the arctic cold of the Wyoming winter, an inversion and great sun exposure keep the wall toasty hot on sunny days.

The Main Wall saw little attention until the early 1990s, when Greg Collins and a small group of other climbers realized the potential that lay before them. Over the ensuing years the route count has grown to over 250, including nearly 50 routes 5.13 and harder. The huge variety of grades, the many different angles, and the consistently good weather make this a prime choice for any season.

DRIVE TIME: 12 minutes from Lander

HIKE: 10 to 15 minutes uphill

SUN EXPOSURE: Sunny until 3 p.m. most of the year

SEASON: Winter, Spring, Fall, and Summer evenings

LENGTH: 40 to 110 feet

MAIN WALL ROUTE COUNT by GRADE								
<5.8	:	10	—	5.9	:	8	—	5.10 : 41
5.11 : 64	—	5.12 : 65	—	5.13 : 40	—	5.14 : 5		

The routes are listed right to left across the entire cliff (numbers 1 to 234), and grouped loosely into sub areas (usually named for that section's best known route).

To help you orient yourself, these sub-areas are marked on the wide-angle panorama across pages 76 & 77.

PANORAMA ABOVE : SINKS CANYON : Main Wall

A. Scud Wall & Pinnacle; **B.** Killer Cave : Right; **C.** Killer Cave : Left;
D. Harvest Moon Wall; **E.** Camel Jockey Wall; **F.** Happy Wheel Wall;
G. The Brisket Wall; **H.** White Heat Wall; **I.** Addiction Wall;
J. Citadel Wall; **K.** Hardware Wall; **L.** Face Dancer Wall; **M.** Moss Cave;
N. Purple Galaxy Wall; **O.** Achin' for Bootie Wall & The Wilds;
P. Squaretop Boulder; **Q.** Wave Mutilation Boulder; **R.** Fairfield Hill.

APPROACH (Main Wall)

The Main Wall is located 2.6 miles from the entrance to the canyon, with the primary parking being on the right side of the road, approximately 100 yards past the cattle guard. Additional parking is available down canyon 1/4 mile on the south side. The trail leaves the primary parking lot from the right corner, and splits after just a few feet at the trailhead sign.

When the parking lot is full PLEASE use the overflow area rather than parking along the road.

Routes 1 to 104 : Follow the right-hand trail, (Killer Cave Trail).
Routes 105 To 234 : Follow the left-hand trail (Addiction Trail).
Routes 235 to 246 : On large boulders below the main cliffs.

The Squaretop Boulder is best reached via parking at the Fairfield Hill road (0.4 miles past the main parking area).
The Wave of Mutilation Boulder can be reached by walking the Addiction Trail to the first switchback, then angling downhill toward the road and around to the south face of the boulder.

Dan McCoy doing his best to *Climb Like a Girl* (10a).
Photo © Ken Driese, 2000.

PORT CLIMBS

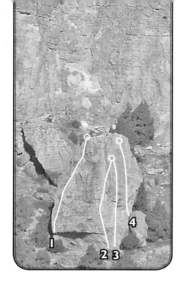

Scud Pinnacle

1. West Ridge 5 (requires gear)
Climb 50 foot prow to web anchors.

2. Spank the Monkey 11d ★
A decent climb up the south side arête. 50 feet

3. Monkeys on the Moon 11c
Take the center of the steep southeast side. 45 feet

4. Monkey Man 10c ★
Climb up off block along seams to a high anchor. 45 feet

Scud Wall

5. Scud Alert 10a
Good pockets up short wall. Left and right variations have been equipped with 2-3 bolts each. Both are silly. 40 feet

6. Storm of the Century 10d ★★
Hard start leads to very good headwall climbing. 55 feet

7. Rubber Soul 11a ★
Easy climbing to tricky bulge. 55 feet

8. Girl's Day Out 6
Face climbing and ledge mantling. 60 feet

9. Mei Day 6
Up corner and low angle face. 60 feet

10. You Go, Girl 10d
Start in corner, then move out onto prow to join *Boy, I Gotta Go*. A bit contrived. 45 feet

11. Boy, I Gotta Go 10a ★★
A very popular prow route. 45 feet

12. Atta Boy, Girl 9 ★

Up pockets and seam to leftward traverse that ends sharing the *Climb Like a Girl* anchors. 50 feet

13. Climb Like a Girl 10a ★

Thin crimps and longer moves, then through small roof above. 50 feet

14. Stud Alert 10c ★★

Move through low overhang to easier slab, then through a 3-foot roof at the top. 50 feet

15. Duck Soup 9 ★★★

Climb up flakes to a steeper wall above. 50 feet

16. Banoffee 10a ★★

Continuous slabby face. 50 feet

17. Doggin' Dude 8 ★

Climb up seam feature to slab above. 50 feet

Killer Cave : Right (see crag photos pages 82 & 83)

18. Action Candy 10a ★★
Long route with many bolts, continuous moderate moves. 80 feet

19. King of Hearts 10d ★
Hard moves low to easy climbing, then through tricky bulge and up slab above. 80 feet

20. Back-up Binkie 12a
Hard bouldery start to easy slab, then up to anchors. 60 feet

21. Second-Hand Nova 11a ★★
Start on thin crimps, moving up and left to a seam. Up face above to small roof. 55 feet

22. Spook Eyes 12b
Start on the right end of big bulge, just behind the big tree. Very powerful start leads to fun, easier climbing to the top. 60 feet

23. Comin' Home Curly 14a
Starts as *One Love*, but break right at bolt three. Hard monos. See photo on Dedication Page. 65 feet

24. One Love 13c ★★
Hard pulls through low bulge, then up vertical wall to another hard roof at the top. 65 feet

25. Endeavor to Stab Bush 13c
This hybrid links the *Endeavor* start to the cruxes of *Clown Stabber* and *Bush Doctor*. 75 feet

26. Endeavor to Persevere 13c ★★★
Climb up center of belly, starting on the big boulder. The hard bit is getting to the undercling crack, then it's just some enduro 13a climbing to the anchors. 75 feet

SINKS CANYON : Main Wall

Neil Humphrey climbing *Action Candy* (10a).
Photo © Ken Driese. January 1997.

PORT CLIMBS

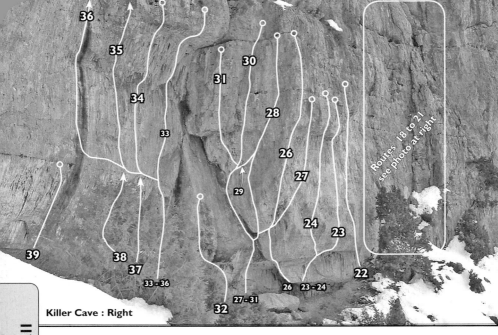

Killer Cave : Right

27. Jimmy Wings Not Included 12c ★

Again, the same start as *Bush Doctor*. After bolt three, traverse right along the undercling, crossing *Endeavor* and turning to the right side of the prow. Up face and through small roof. Not as contrived as it sounds, and pretty fun. 70 feet

28. Clown Stabber 12d ★

Same start as *Bush Doctor*, then right into bulge after bolt three. Long moves to easy corner above. 75 feet

29. Bloodline 11d ★★

Same as *Bush Doctor*, but traverses right to a big dihedral after bolt six (This route actually is a combo of *Bush Doctor* and *Clown Stabber*). 75 feet

30. Bush Doctor 12a ★★★

Start in a major corner above a big boulder. If the start is done from the ground (*sans* cheater blocks/log) this route is 12b. Climb up corner, through bulge, then straight up after bolt six. 75 feet

31. Ring of Fire 12c ★

Shares the *Bush Doctor* start, but moves left after bolt six, through the small roof and up a steep prow. 75 feet

Killer Cave : Right

21   20   19 18

22

17

Paul Piana on *Clown Stabber*, (12d).
Photo © Ken Driese.

PORT CLIMBS

32. The Urchin 13a ★★

Short and powerful route, starts in undercling/lieback corner, up and over bulge. 45 feet

33. Project.

Climbs up *Baghdad's* corner, then straight up and out the big roof above. 75 feet

34. Baghdad 12c ★

Climb left-facing corner to horizontal, traverse left and up big holds through steep wall above. 75 feet

35. Basra 12c

Start as for *Baghdad*, but continue left along horizontal to next line of bolts. Climb up and through steeps above. 80 feet

36. House of God 13a

Start in *Baghdad's* left-facing corner, up to horizontal pocket band, then left all the way to black streak and up. 100 feet

37. Shao Lin Shadow Boxing 13b

Hard pulls between positive holds. Join *Baghdad* to finish. 80 feet

38. Organics 14b ★

Start in underclings, moving left and up steep wall to horizontal band. Join *Basra* to the top. 80 feet

39. Virga 13c ★

Tram start. Short route that moves past hard pulls, ending at anchor near horizontal band of pockets. 4 bolts, 35 feet

BJ Tilden on the FA of *Organics* (14b).
Photo © Steve Bechtel.

Unknown climber on *Nirvana* (13a).
Photo © David Anderson.

PORT CLIMBS

Killer Cave : Left

See Crag Photo on
Page 88

40. Kingdom of Jah 12c/d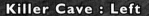

Share start with *Cartoon*,
but traverse even further right,
then up good pockets to anchors
just left of black streak. 75 feet

41. Nirvana 13a ⭐⭐

Same start as *Cartoon*, but continue
right where *Cartoon* goes straight up. Long
moves up a continuously steep wall. 85 feet

SINKS CANYON : Main Wall

Jed Workman climbing *Killer* **(12c)**.
Photo © David Anderson

42. Samsara 13b ★★★

Climb *Cartoon Graveyard* to the horizontal rest, then up and right through roof. 90 feet

43. Cartoon Graveyard 12d ★★★

A0 start (at ring bolt and standard hanger) to undercling, then up right through low crux. After rest go straight up to anchors below six foot roof. The extension through the roof is *Exodus*. 80 feet

44. Exodus 13c ★★

A three-bolt extension to *Cartoon Graveyard* that adds substantially to the difficulty. 90 feet

45. Stronger Than Reason 13b/c ★

Hard thin pockets straight up from the *Killer* start bolt. Joins *Mr. Majestyk* at high horizontal. 90 feet

46. Mr. Majestyk 13a ★★★

Up *Killer* to the end of the seam, then right through 12a crux, up corner to good rest. Punch it through steep climbing to horizontal, and up left to share *Sweet Bro* anchors. **Mrs. Majestyk** is a 12c variation that traverses right to the *Cartoon Graveyard* anchors before the crux lip moves. 90 feet

47. Sweet Bro 13a ★

Takes *Killer* to just above the roof, then moves right and up hard long moves, then over roof at top. 90 feet

48. Killer 12c ★★

A0 start (usually a fixed aider on bolt one) to gain seam, follow it left and up to juggy wall and roof above. 80 feet

49. The Successor 13b ★★

Thin moves up seam feature, then up continuous difficulties to roof at top. 80 feet

50. The Throne 13a ★★★

Hard crimping leads to an undercling, then long moves up headwall. 80 feet

51. Wield the Scepter 13c ★

Starts just right of *Busload*, traverses hard undercling arch into *The Throne*, then up that route. See photo page 16. 85 feet

52. Busload of Faith 14a ★★

Hard moves from the get-go. 60 feet

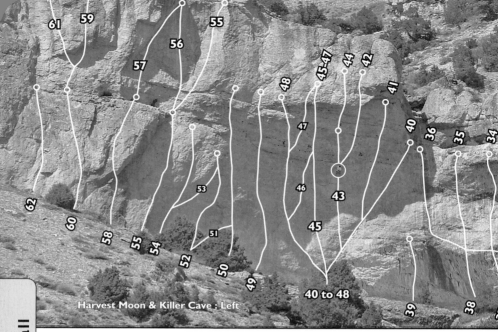

Harvest Moon & Killer Cave : Left

53. Sister Ray 13a

Start as for *Moonstone*, but head right and join the upper section of *Busload of Faith*. 60 feet

54. Moonstone 13b ★★

Climb up hard moves to a great jug, past more hard moves, and up easier terrain. This climb follows a beautiful golden streak. 70 feet

55. Blue Moon 12a ★★

Great climbing up big flake and through overhanging terrain above. Sporty. This route originally went to the top of the cliff, but is now done to anchors after bolt six. 70 feet

56. To the Moon, Alice 12b ★

Continue straight up the wall above the lower half of *Blue Moon*, heading for the top of *Cutthroat*. This is a very high route, use care in lowering! 50 feet

57. Cutthroat 11d

The big leaning corner above *Brown Trout*. Use care in lowering if climbing this route from the ground; a 60 meter rope will barely get you down. 45 feet

58. Brown Trout 11c

Unfortunately a little wet, but good climbing through diagonal roof. 85 feet

59. Hypernova 12b ★★★

From the end of *Sign of the Times* pitch one, climb up and right to roof then over and up shallow corner. Use caution when lowering! 105 feet

Steve Babits climbing *Brown Trout* (11c).
Photo © David Anderson.

SINKS CANYON : Main Wall

SINKS CANYON : Main Wall

60. Sign of the Times 11b

`P1` Technical climbing up and left to chain anchor. 50 feet

61. Sign of the Times 13a ★

`P2` Up black streak in headwall above chains.

Total length is 105 feet. Be careful on rappel/lower.

62. Powderfinger 11a ★

Follow seam to big flake, then up and over to jugs above. 6 bolts, 50 feet

63. After the Goldrush 11c ★★

Climbs thin face to easier pocketed headwall. An alternate start traverses in from *Harvest Moon* at 5.10b (**Harvest Rush**). 7 bolts, 60 feet

64. Harvest Moon 11a ★★

Start up rightward undercling, then straight up on glassy holds. Features ring-type bolts. Continuous. 55 feet

LANDER S

65. Sun Spot 11d ★

Climb up slick crimps and small pockets to good holds near the top. 45 feet

66. Firecracker Kid 10b ★★

Up lieback flake, then traverse left to corner climbing. 55 feet

67. Elmo's Fish 10d ★★

Climb up shallow corner to undercling and up steep face. 60 feet

68. Pocket Calculator 12b ★

Starts just left of large bush, up thin pockets to long easier wall above. 60 feet

69. Global Warm-Up 10c ★

Begin in small corner, and up to less steep terrain. 6 bolts, 45 feet

Lee Brown climbing *Harvest Moon* **(11a).**
Photo © Steve Bechtel.

Camel Jockey Wall

70. Put Down Your Ducky 8 ★★

Exceedingly popular slab route. 80 feet

71. The Ogre 11a

Short route just right of a small gully. No photo. 30 feet

72. Red Light Love 11c ★

Start on flakes, up right, then fun moves to anchor. 65 feet

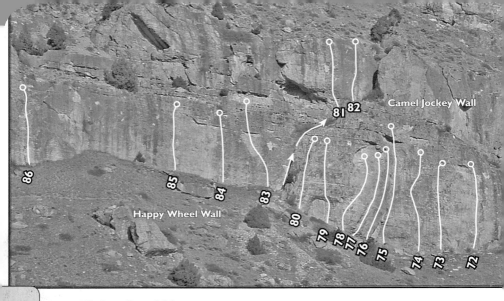

73. Lost Boy 12d
Burly thin climbing. 50 feet

74. Child's Play 10c ★
Flakes to thin crux, then up and right to anchors. 55 feet

75. More Funky Than Gunky 9 ★★
Very popular crack in corner then up through small roof. 70 feet

76. Camel Jockey 13b ★
Up center of pretty wall on long moves. 60 feet

77. Sand Digger 12b ★★
Start on hard boulder problem into crack, then up steep face to hard exit moves. 65 feet

78. Wammoe 12b/c
Continuously hard moves up vertical wall. 60 feet

79. Straight Up Crew 11c ★
Up right side of small arch, then through bulge to slab. 50 feet

80. No Self Control 10c
Thin slab climbing. 45 feet

81. Spent Rods 11b

This route and *Bad Milk* begin on the ledge up behind No Self *Control*. Climb up gully to left to reach the ledge. 35 feet

82. Bad Milk 11a

The right route on the upper ledge, this climb is the better of the two. 35 feet

83. Bones Brigade 10a

Climb up face into left-trending corner. 65 feet

84. Hunger Force 11c

Climb off flake into hard crux, then up easier moves to top. Sharp. 45 feet

85. Dogtown 9 ★

Climb a right-facing corner to big holds. 45 feet

86. Z-Boys 8 ★★

Follows fun flakes up a low-angle wall. 50 feet

The Brisket Wall

Happy Wheel Wall

PORT CLIMBS

Ken Driese on *The Brisket* (12c). February 1992.
Photo © Ken Driese Collection.

LANDER S

87. White Lotus 13c ★
Climbs steep rock on off-balance moves. 45 feet

88. Twice Baked 11c
Takes the prow right of *Happy Wheel*. 50 feet

89. Happy Wheel 10a ★
Start in well-protected corner, then move out of corner to right and up face. 45 feet

90. Where They Gonna Run When Destruction Comes? 12c ★
Up difficult face to hard high bulge. 70 feet

91. Cloud Calling 12b
Climb the dark streak up a gently overhanging wall. Traverse left to *Yellow Cake* anchors. 50 feet

92. Yellow Cake 12b
Thin moves, hard mono, and an easier top. 50 feet

93. Pet Arête 10d
Balancy arête to spicy rightward traverse at top. Shares *Yellow Cake* anchors. 50 feet

The Brisket Wall

See Crag Photos on Pages 93 & 96

94. Pigs in Zen 11a
Very short red slab, right side. 30 feet

95. Caught Stealing 10b
Very short red slab, left side. 30 feet

96. Praying to the Aliens 10b ★
Climbs an awkward crack system to anchors just below big ledge. 35 feet

97. Rokai Corner 8 ★
Fun, easy climbing up polished corner. 40 feet

98. The Guyver 10b ★★
Follow thin seam and face to anchors near a small roof. 45 feet

99. Fine Dining 12b ★
Seams and thin edges right of *Brisket*. 45 feet

SPORT CLIMBS

100. The Brisket 12c
Very bouldery climbing up seam, then left and up face. 45 feet

101. Angel of Mercy 11a ★
This route follows the big corner crack, then moves left to share the last half with *Guardian Angel*. 75 feet

102. Guardian Angel 12a
Thin face moves on wall left of big corner to fun headwall above. 75 feet

103. Pocket Full of Kryptonite 13b
Hard thin climbing to a one-bolt anchor. 50 feet

104. Titanic 11b ★
Climbs left-facing corner to ledge, then through bulge and up long face above. 100 feet

LANDER S

Rio Rose climbing *White Heat* (12d).
Photo © David Anderson.

PORT CLIMBS

White Heat Wall

105. Little Creatures 11b ★★
Traverse ledge right to the beginning of this route. Hard thin moves lead to fun, pumpy climbing above. Be careful lowering off if your rope is less than 60 meters. 85 feet

106. Peter Bopp 11a ★
Up face/seam to hard headwall. 80 feet

107. Hale Bopp 10d ★
Climbs low-angle face to progressively steeper wall. Baffling crux at top. 80 feet

108. Storm Warning 9 ★★
Climb up edges and seams to right side of bulge, then over it to a ledge and up vertical wall above. 80 feet

109. Spike n' Vein 11b ★★★
Similar to *No Impact* but with an easier slab and easier bulge. 50 feet

110. No Impact 11d ★★
Hard slab climbing leads to big moves through bulge. 50 feet

111. Searching for Jose Cuervo 12b ★★
Climb up tricky slab to bulge, trough bulge on thin pockets, then up fun headwall. 80 feet

112. Central Pillar 11a ★
Climb up tall "pillar", then past thin moves into left-facing corner feature. Up past ledge to fun headwall. 80 feet

113. Consumption 12b ★
Continuously difficult moves between small holds. 50 feet

114. Project. The Sting
Very thin crimping on a nearly blank wall. 50 feet

115. War Party 12b
Low crux in seam, leads to easier climbing. 50 feet

116. Blushing Crow 12c ★★
Shares start with *White Heat*, moves right and up long moves between good pockets. 55 feet

L A N D E R S

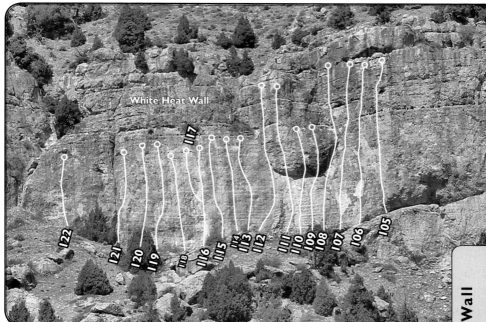

White Heat Wall

117. White Heat 12d ★★
Start in small left-facing corner, the up and left to huecos. Hard moves from these lead to easier climbing. 55 feet

118. Project. Acid Ranger
Looks really hard. Thin crimps, long moves. 50 feet

119. Mono a Mono 13a ★
Long moves between monos. 50 feet

120. Dime Time 13a
Hateful crimps up vertical wall. 50 feet

121. Fun, Fun, Joy, Joy 10b ★
Climbs up corner then out onto face to the right. 50 feet

122. Shortie Sortie 10c
Up center of slab right of Addiction Wall. 40 feet

Cathryn Brodie on *Little Creatures*, (11b).
Photo Opposite © Ken Driese.

Frank Dusl having a *War Party* (12b).
Photo © Ken Driese. March 1992.

LANDER

See Crag Photo on Page 103

123. Dewalt's Challenge 11d

Steep climbing up flakes and edges. Tends to collect a bit of dirt from runoff. 25 feet

124. The Black Hole 12d ★

Hard steep moves past obvious "black hole" pocket. 35 feet

125. White Dwarf 12c ★★

Continuous hard moves up bulging wall. 40 feet

Wendy Davis climbing *Dogs of War* (13b).
Photo © David Anderson.

PORT CLIMBS

126. Corner Drug 11a ★★
The chalked up corner climb. Pumpy. 55 feet

127. Drug Enemy 11d ★★
Climbs *Corner Drug* to third bolt, then traverses left on jugs to finish on *Public Enemy*. 65 feet

128. Public Enemy 12c ★
Climb up thin seam to good rest, then through short high crux at top. 70 feet

129. The Gathering 13b/c ★★
Steep climbing on crimps. 70 feet

130. Pretty Hate Machine 13b ★★★
Directly behind the big tree. Long, hard moves. 75 feet

131. Dogs of War 13b ★★
Hard barn-door moves to crimp crux. 75 feet

132. Addiction 12c ★★★
Climb up and right on crimps to a good rail, then up long moves to a final slab crux. 70 feet

133. Surplus Fusion Reaction 13a ★★
Steep face left of *Addiction*, crimps and small pockets. 65 feet

134. Soul Finger 11a ★
Starts as for *Mezzmerie*, but moves right and up corner. 55 feet

135. Mezzmerie 12c
Climbs up seam to small ledge, then out left onto face. 45 feet

136. Go West, Young Man 6 ★★★
Climb left-arcing crack. 45 feet

137. Soup Sandwich 8 ★
Slab to *Go West* anchors. 40 feet

138. A Beautiful Life 9 ★★
Follow flakes and seam up slab. Named in memory of Jim Ratz. 45 feet

139. Black Celebration 11b
On high wall above and left of Addiction wall. Black streak. 30 feet

SINKS CANYON : Main Wall

Addiction Wall

Gully to Top

approach trail

Leif Gasch climbing *Pretty Hate Machine* (13b).
Photo © David Anderson.

103

PORT CLIMBS

Tarris Webber climbing *Dogs of War* (13b).
Photo © David Anderson.

LANDER

140. The Earth Died Screaming 12b

Easier climbing leads to long hard headwall moves. 75 feet

141. The Stronghold of Decay 12c ★

Work up thin, sometimes dirty moves, past a few really cool holds. 75 feet

142. Citadel of Hope 12b ★★★

Climb up and right on good holds to horizontal, then up through twisty, fun moves. 75 feet

143. Divine Intervention 13b ★

Climb *Citadel* to horizontal, then up and left on very small holds. 75 feet

144. West of Hell 13b ★★

Lower-angled face to crimpy headwall. Ends beneath large block. 75 feet

145. Paladin 12a ★

Stout crimping leads to long headwall moves. 75 feet

The Citadel

SINKS CANYON : Main Wall

Kirk Billings climbing *Citadel of Hope* (12b).
Photo © David Anderson.

LANDER

146. Tel Aviv Miracle 12b ★★

Relentless crimping leads to a good rest, then a tricky finishing move. 50 feet

147. Right About Now 11c ★★

Hard face climbing to BIG jug, then up steep wall to easy slab finish. 70 feet

148. Funk Soul Brother 12a ★

Easier vertical face leads to horizontal break with tricky climbing above. 70 feet

149. Blood Brother 11a ★★★

Climb ramp to vertical face that leads to slightly overhanging seam. (see photo pages 10-11). 75 feet

150. Wide Awake Zombie 12b

Climbs face just left of *Blood Brother*. Difficult to stay left of *Blood Brother* at crux. 75 feet

151. Fun Planet 10a ★

Follows slab to high right-facing dihedral on left side of Citadel Wall. 70 feet

152. Biltong Rides Tornado 10c ★★

Just right of *Fat Boys*, fun climbing up steep wall. 50 feet

153. Fat Boys Skip School 11a

Begins on ledge system reached by scrambling up from right. Climbs up flakes and pockets to high crux. 50 feet

Hardware Wall

The Citadel

Hardware Wall ──────────────────

154. Value Pack 12b
Climbs up ledge systems to high crux on wall right of *Postcards* flake. 80 feet

155. Project. Anchor bolts only.

156. Postcards From the Edge 11d
Follow short arête on detached block to anchors. 30 feet

157. Mutt and Jeff 11b ★★
Shares the start chimney of *Heaven Can Wait*, then moves right and up well-protected face above. 80 feet

158. Heaven Can Wait 11c ★★
A chimney to a leftward traverse joining *The Heavens*. 75 feet

159. The Heavens 13b ★
Hard moves lead to a good rest, then 5.11 climbing to the top. 75 feet

160. First Responder 13b ★★
Thin climbing up to scoop, then up, up, up to high crux. 90 feet

SINKS CANYON : Main Wall

Hardware Wall

LANDERS

161. Murgatroid 12a ★★

Hard edge climbing leads to a good rest in a scoop, followed by easier, but continuous climbing above. 80 feet

162. Angry Bob 12c ★

Climbs crimps up gold streak. 60 feet

163. Upheaval 13b ★★

Long pulls lead up and right toward *Angry Bob*. 70 feet

164. Mark 13 13a ★★

Follows seams to long reaches between crimps. 70 feet

165. Software 12c

A direct start to the top of *Hardware*, usually a bit damp. 65 feet

166. Hardware 12a ★★

Climb up thin crack to a rightward traverse, then up easier climbing to top. Chalked sidepulls mark the start. 65 feet

Bryon Bennett on *Hardware* (12a). Photo © Ken Driese.

167. Jill 12d ★

A desperate crimp move leads to easier climbing above. 65 feet

168. Mo 12b/c ★★

Begin in a left-facing lieback with lots of chalk. Large crimps and jugs. Very fun, but with a couple of somewhat greasy holds at the top. 60 feet

169. Shades 12d ★★

Steep small crimps, continuous. 60 feet

170. The Zone 13b ★

Crimp your way to the top. 60 feet

171. Slippery People 12b

Poor. "Trouty" damp rock makes for a disappointing climb. 60 feet

172. Milkman 13a ★★

Bouldery movement on edges and small pockets. 60 feet

173. The Evil One 13a ★

Climb right on "ramp" hold, then past savage moves to anchor. 60 feet

174. No Left Ear 10d ★ or 11d

Up well-protected juggy face to anchors, or continue through very hard roof. 75 feet

175. Whipperly Wamberly Walk 11b ★★

Climb up ledges to a small overhang, then up tough moves to jugs. Follow good holds up and over the high roof. 75 feet

176. Apple City Quick Step 11b

Up slab to interesting roof. 75 feet

Face Dancer Wall ────────────────────

177. Billie Idol 10c

Climbs up the easy south face of the leaning pillar (see photo right), then up good pockets on the main wall above. 75 feet

178. Kamiakin 10b ★

Start on blocky ledge just left of the leaning pillar. 65 feet

179. No More Heroes 10c

Hard low to easy climbing up slab. 60 feet

180. Fallen Idol 11b

Hard move low to easy slab above. 65 feet

181. Wind River Rose 11a

Begins just above jumbled boulders, a bit dirty. 70 feet

182. Wicker Man 11b

Sharp climbing. Go right at top. 75 feet

183. Eros 10d ★★

Climb up and right on rails and pockets. 85 feet

184. Face Dancer 11b ★★★

Popular route leads up big flake/slab to vertical wall with glassy pockets. 85 feet

185. Winds of War 10c ★★

Start up ramp, then follow sustained moves to anchors. 85 feet

186. Diemos 10d ★★

Up gray slab, then through fun moves to a right-facing corner near the top. 85 feet

LANDERS

187. Blessed Saint Yabo 11c ★★

Begins with the same bouldery move as *Stone Seed*, but moves straight up where *Stone Seed* traverses left. 50 feet

188. Stone Seed 11d ★ (2 short pitches)

Hard moves off pointy flakes at bottom to rail, then traverse left and up to anchors. A second, easier, pitch leads higher. 80 feet

189. Calling Saint Fiacre 11c ★

Climb small pillar/corner to hard moves that lead into the end of *Stone Seed*. 60 feet

Photo © Ken Driese.

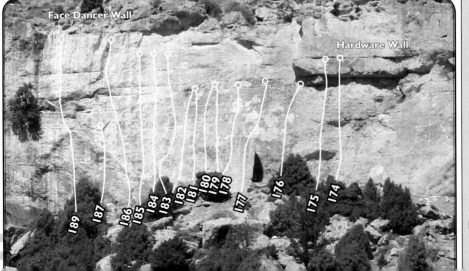

Face Dancer Wall

Hardware Wall

189 187 186 185 184 183 182 181 180 179 178 177 176 175 174

Steve Bechtel in the Moss Cave.

Moss Cave

190. Skinny Fat Man 12d ★
Takes the gray steak on the rightmost side of the Moss Cave. Technical. 6 bolts, 65 feet

191. Smoke Shapes 13d/14a ★★
Jump start to monos up streak. 55 feet

192. Project. The Man

193. Project. The Man They Couldn't Hang

194. Confession of a Mask 12d ★★★
A0 Tram start leads to long moves between generally good holds.

195. Project. Pogey Bait

196. Good Luck Mr. Gorsky 13c ★★
A0 Tram start. Hard pulls on continuously steep wall.

197. Touchy Feely 11d
Climb up the left side of a white streak, about 50 feet after the trail exits the small "forest". See photo opposite page. 70 feet

Face Dancer Wall

Moss Cave

193 196 195 194 192 191 190 189 188 187 186 185 184 183 182 181 180 179 178 177 176

LANDER

———— Purple Galaxy Wall (see photo on next page)

198. Bush Fire 12a ★
Good climb up rust streak on right side of clean wall. 50 feet

199. Crowheart 12b/c ★★
Good route up center of wall. Same anchors as *Macumba*. 50 feet

200. Macumba 11d
Thin and sharp face, just right of *Southpaw* crack. 50 feet

201. Southpaw 10c ★★
Climb a left-leaning undercling crack, exiting onto face above. 50 feet

202. Monkey in the White House 11d
Follows light-colored rock from top of flake/ledge. 45 feet

203. Cheese Wheel 12b
Slab behind tree, trend left at the start. 50 feet

204. Purple Galaxy 12a ★★★
A hard opening sequence leads to a good rest; then up tough moves to a horizontal. Either lower from anchors here (11d, 80 feet) or continue three more bolts to the top. 100 feet

205. Project.
206. Aqualung 11c
Climb a big left-facing corner and up the face above. 60 feet

207. Gongoozled 11d ★★
Continuous tricky moves, then through a hard bulge at the top. 85 feet

208. Grabbing Greta 11c ★
Start in a left-facing corner, moves left to difficult moves on a slab, then climb through a bulge near the top.

209. Parts and Labor 11b
Take the slab up to steeper climbing, then through a small roof at the top. 90 feet

Achin' for Bootie Wall

See Crag Photo on Page 116

210. Waiting on a Friend 11b ★★

A difficult entry move leads to fun jug pulling and a small bulge above. 80 feet

211. Smell My Finger 11d ★★

Climb face right of *Achin'* to crack feature at top. Pumpy. 90 feet

212. Achin' for Bootie 11d ★★★

Climb up right-facing corner to a small ledge with a chain bolt. Move straight up the center of the face to a high crux. 95 feet

213. Cavity Search 11d ★

Slab to lieback crack, then hard bulge before headwall. 90 feet

214. Picture of Industry 11c ★★
Climb a crack feature up to a bulge, then through it and up to anchors near a small bush. 85 feet

215. Ride the Apocalypse 12b ★
Climb up blocky rock behind a tree to a very hard move, followed by 5.10 climbing to the anchors. 70 feet

216. Brrravery 12b
Up right-trending seam to "bling" chain anchor. 65 feet

217. Opal 12a
Up the face just left of a small corner, then through a mini roof to anchor on the arête above. 65 feet

218. Renaissance Man 8
Up prow/slab on sharp rock. 60 feet

219. Bust A Nut 11b ★★
Climb up small pillar to discontinuous cracks. Follow cracks and good moves to anchor below the large square-cut roof. 50 feet

220. Bump-N-Grind 12a
Follows deceptive prow to anchors below large square-cut roof. 50 feet

221. Spragglepuss 10c
Low angle climbing behind large pine. Techy. 45 feet

PORT CLIMBS

The Wilds

222. Combustification 11a ★
Double cracks. 55 feet

223. The Physical 12c ★
Hard moves to groove, continuing difficulty, steep top out. 6 bolts, 50 feet

224. Snap Back Relax 13a
Boulder problem start to easier moves. 50 feet

225. Wicked Garden 9
Chossy gully. 55 feet

226. Project. Mind Over Matter
227. Savages 13a ★★
Good thin climbing up nice wall, just left of obvious hueco. 50 feet

228. The Wilds 12a ★★
Start up small left-facing corner, then up hard moves above.

229. Get on With It 12b ★★
Hard, thin climbing. Technical.

230. Sandman 10c ★★
Up thin right-facing flake system to steeper wall above.

231. Tooth Fairy 10c ★
Techy face climbing, starting in small groove. Continuous.

232. Ankle Biter 10d
Up low angle rock to rightward traverse near top.

233. Candyman 10d ★
The leftmost route on the wall. Climb up easy left-facing corner/
flake system to ledge (5.5), then up steep wall above. 60 feet

234. Earth A.D. 10a
Dirty slab at very left end of cliff. 40 feet

Squaretop Boulder

See photo on page 76-77 for an overview location of Squaretop.

APPROACH (Squaretop Boulder)

The Squaretop Boulder is best reached via parking at the Fairfield Hill road (0.4 miles past the main parking area). See page 121 for details.

---

235. Girly 5.11d
Steep wall left of the *German Girl* arête. 4 bolts, 35 feet

236. German Girl 12c
The steep and cool looking overhanging arête. 40 feet

237. Burly 11d ★★
A semi-classic. Jug haul it up the west face right of the arête. 40 feet

238. Boys From Brazil 11c
Steep corner and face right of *Burly*. 40 feet

239. Full Irations 12a
The left route on the SE face, start off boulder to reachy moves. 30 feet

240. Zion Train 12b ★★
Good pockets up center of face. 35 feet

241. EZ Up 10c
Hard start leads to easy climbing above. 40 feet

242. Darksides 12b TR
Face left of dihedral. 30 feet

243. Original Route 9
Bolted corner on north side. 35 feet

244. Crack Variation 11a
Toprope or protect with poor gear. 35 feet

LANDER S

South Side

236 237 238 239 240

North Side

241 242 243 244 235 236

SPORT CLIMBS

Wave of Mutilation Boulder

See photo on page 76-77 for an overview location of this boulder.

APPROACH (Wave of Mutilation Boulder)

The Wave of Mutilation Boulder can be reached by walking the Addiction Trail to the first switchback, then angling downhill toward the road and around to the south face of the rock.

245. Monkey Gone To Heaven 14b ★★

The left route on the Wave of Mutilation Boulder. Monos, etc. 25 feet

246. Wave of Mutilation 13c ★★

Long moves between good pockets. Steep! 30 feet

LANDER S

SINKS CANYON : Fairfield Hill

The Fairfield Hill cliff is the westernmost developed dolomite cliff in Sinks Canyon. Fairfield has always been the black sheep of Sinks Canyon climbing. Although development here has paralleled that of the Main Wall, it has received only a fraction the traffic. Development here has included several climbers; but, well over half of the nearly 80 climbs were established by Bob Branscomb. His efforts, and the efforts of Ed Delong, Paul Piana, Dave Doll, and a few others have created one of the finest crags in Wyoming.

DRIVE TIME: 15 minutes from Lander

HIKE: 20 to 30 minutes uphill

SUN EXPOSURE: Sunny until 4 p.m.

SEASON: Spring, Fall, Summer evenings

LENGTH: 40 to 80 feet

FAIRFIELD ROUTE COUNT by GRADE

<5.9 : 14 — **5.10 :** 17 — **5.11 :** 25 — **5.12 :** 11 — **5.13 :** 3

PARKING & APPROACH (Fairfield Hill)

Drive up canyon 3 miles from the "Entering Sinks Canyon State Park" sign, and take the two-track on the right. If you have a low clearance vehicle, it may be best to park just off the pavement and walk. Follow this road for three-quarters of a mile and park. Walk up the very rough 4WD road above for about 250 yards to a right-hand trail marked by two large cairns. Follow this long diagonal all the way to the right end of the Fairfield Hill cliff. From here a climbers' trail leads back west (left) along the base.

Routes are described from right to left.

This is also a good approach trail for the left end of the Sinks Main Wall. An obvious trail connects the Fairfield and Main Walls near the top of the long diagonal of the Fairfield approach trail.

Fairfield East Wall

1. Hieroglyphic 11c ★
The right route on the pinnacle; rightmost route on Fairfield Hill. Takes center of steep face. No photo. 55 feet

2. Kissing Marilyn Monroe 11c
On left side of the arête of "pinnacle" formation; turn arête at bolt four. 50 feet

3. They Shoot Horses 11b ★
On face of pinnacle; begins with left-hand sidepulls. 50 feet

4. Con's West Right 6
The right-hand slab uphill and west of the pinnacle. 25 feet

5. Con's West Left 10a
The left slab. 3 bolts, 25 feet

6. Top Rope 10b
Slab with long chain anchor. 30 feet

7. Apostrophe 10a
Shares bolt one with *Treats*. 40 feet

8. Treats 9 ★
Harder than the others, but really fun. 40 feet

9. Revenge of the Pygmy Sex God 8 ★
Short, but fun.

10. Realm of the Venusian Sex Pygmies 7
Nice easy climb.

11. West of Venus 7
Nice slab. 45 feet

12. Say Hello To Geronimo 10b ★★
Through little bulge to easy slab above. 6 bolts, 50 feet

13. A Piolet for Leon 10d ★
Thin and tricky face climbing. 50 feet

14. Che 11d ★
Similar to previous route. 50 feet

15. Leon Trotsky's Hair 11c ★
Thin crimping up nice face. 60 feet

16. Sorta Maybe Kinda Wild 10b ★★
Corner to face traverse right. Shares anchors with *Leon Trotsky's Hair*. 60 feet

17. Project.
Three bolts to anchors up blunt arête.

PORT CLIMBS

East Wall : Left Side

18. Big Bambu 11b
Long moves past 3 bolts on slightly overhanging wall. 35 feet

19. Blind 11d
Vertical wall with big flakes. 75 feet

20. Project.
Dark streak right of arches.

21. Presence 10d ★
Dark wall starting near grey bushes. 50 feet

22. Houses of the Holy 10b ★★
Good slab route, starts behind junipers. 50 feet

23. Physical Graffiti 11a ★
Tricky climbing. 45 feet

24. Your Own Private Idaho 10c ★
Good slab climbing beneath big boulder at rim. 45 feet

25. L, L, & L 8
Leftmost route on white slab. 35 feet

26. Meadow rock TRs
Several short top ropes between Central and Right sectors.

LANDERS

27. World On A String 11b
Tricky and sharp. 40 feet

28. Hanoi Jane's Video Workout 11a
Up face and into crack with tree. 40 feet

29. Brave Like Old John Wayne 11d ★
Tech climbing on left end of black vertical wall. 40 feet

30. Beef Pudding 12c ★
Right route on east-facing block. 40 feet

31. Zebra Cakes 12b ★★
Left side of east-facing block. 40 feet

Fairfield Central Wall

32. Straight, No Chaser 10b
Climbs long arête/flake feature. 60 feet

33. Exile on Main Street 12a ★
Sustained climbing on small holds. 65 feet

34. Electric Fence 12b ★★
Up clean white face and through the high bulges. 75 feet

35. Hellzapoppin 11d ★★
Start in right-facing corner, up clean wall, and finish through bulge at top. 70 feet

36. Nobody's Fault But Mine 10b
Good short route. 35 feet

37. I Wish I Was A Catfish 10c
Similar to nearby routes. 40 feet

38. Atom Tan 10c ★
A good and techy climb. 40 feet

39. Jump Jim Crow 11b ★
Continuous difficulty. 40 feet

40. Have Mercy 10c ★
Tricky slab. 40 feet

41. Visualize Whirled Peas 10b ★★
Another short route, really fun. 35 feet

42. Last Trip To Tulsa 8 ★
Short and fun. 35 feet

43. Coyote Delight 7
Decent and cleaner than most Fairfield routes. 40 feet

44. Uncle Meat 8
Sporty but good holds. 40 feet

45. Youth Culture Killed My Dog 9 ★
Best of these routes. 45 feet

46. Born Cross-Eyed 10a ★
Left-trending slab route. 45 feet

47. Screaming Trees 11a ★
Challenging and sporty route just right of *Chainsaw Willy*, starts behind juniper. 50 feet

48. Chainsaw Willy 10d ★★
Climb left-leaning crack to face above. 50 feet

49. Touch of Gray 10c ★★
Well-protected route just left of small prow. 45 feet

50. Alan Shepard Goes to Space 11b ★
Starts in overlaps right of big juniper. 65 feet

51. Saucerful of Secrets 11d ★★
Good route up clean vertical wall. End at 3-bolt anchor. 60 feet

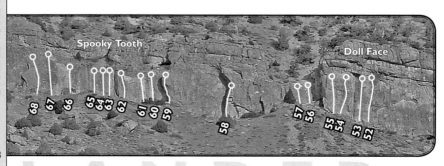

SINKS CANYON : Fairfield Hill

52. Our Barbies, Ourselves 12a ★
Improbable line up overhanging wall. 70 feet

53. Doll Parts 11d ★
Climb up steep terrain and then up right side of corner. 70 feet

54. Doll Face 13b ★★
Curving line on right side of clean steep wall. 70 feet

55. My Dying Bride 12d ★
Takes the left side of the beautiful steep face. 65 feet

56. Tweedle Dum 6
The right short face. 25 feet

57. Tweedle Dee 5
Left of two short faces. 25 feet

Spooky Tooth Wall

58. Kashmir 11a
Takes arête and face to disappointingly low anchors. 45 feet

59. Viatameen H 12d ★★
Sprint route on nice steep prow. 35 feet

60. A Dream of Least Weasels 12b ★★
Thin holds, great rock. 35 feet

61. Save a Prayer For Lefty 13b ★
Follow a left leaning flake to hard high face moves. 35 feet

62. Shadowline 11b
Tricky climbing up rounded arête. 40 feet

63. Manifest Destiny 10a
Great climbing for a little route. 30 feet

64. Axis of Weasel 12a
Another thin route on pretty rock. 35 feet

65. Weasels Ripped My Flesh 12a
Follows pretty black streak. 40 feet

SINKS CANYON : Fairfield Hill

SPORT CLIMBS

66. Moveable Feast 9
Up lieback flake. 45 feet

67. The Great Deceiver 11b
Pretty reddish face right of the big tooth. 50 feet

68. Spooky Tooth 7
Flake climb. Right side. The left side of this flake is 5.5 and is done with gear. 4 bolts, 45 feet

SINKS CANYON : Fairfield Hill

LANDER S

The Roof is about 50 yards left of the route *Spooky Tooth*.

69. Swift 11a
Face left of small roof, conservatively protected with 3 bolts. 45 feet

70. Driller's Delight 11d
Up left leaning crack feature to vertical climbing above. 45 feet

71. The Abortion 11d
Thin face moves to turn big roof at its very right side. 50 feet

72. Project.
Roof projects.

73. The Plague 12c
Clean face just right of red rock. 3 bolts to chain anchor. 40 feet

74. Sensor 11c
Dark wall, thin slab. 3 bolts, 35 feet

The Bubble Wall

The Bubble Wall is about 100 yards left of the route *Sensor*.

75. Fizzle Doubt 12c ★★

Up overhanging face right of the main "bubble." 50 feet

76. Sheepeater 13a ★

Through center of bulge.

77. Don Ho 12b ★★★

Takes left side of bulge. 50 feet

78. Project.

Left side of Bubble Wall. Anchors only.

The Joint is the first of the granite cliffs on the right side of the Middle Fork Trail, near the end of the paved road. The newest and the most concentrated of the developed granite crags in upper Sinks, it is the only one described here although the extensive features farther up canyon have a few routes. The Joint is characterized by steep ground separated by distinct ledges. The Fun House ledge is reached by climbing any number of routes on the lower tier. A few protection bolts are in place to safegaurd climbers moving back and forth along the ledge.

DRIVE TIME: 15 minutes from Lander

HIKE: 15 minutes uphill

SUN EXPOSURE: Sunny until 2 p.m. most of the year

SEASON: Spring, Fall, and Summer evenings

LENGTH: 40 to 150 feet

THE JOINT ROUTE COUNT by GRADE

5.9 : 1 — **5.10** : 2 — **5.11** : 8 — **5.12** : 6 — **5.13** : 3

The Joint, as seen from Bruce's Parking Area.

The Fun House, 11c

Ledge

Main Wall

Right Side

PARKING & APPROACH (The Joint)

The Joint is reached by parking at the "Bruce's Parking Area" just after the road crosses the river (4.2 miles from the canyon entrance). There are toilets at the Parking Area. Cross the road to the foot bridge and cross the river. Head up canyon about 5 minutes along the Middle Fork Trail. The cliff is visible for the entire approach. About 200 feet after passing the last electrical pole along the trail, angle up right and scramble to the cliff via talus slopes. Cairns mark most of this path.

To Joint : Main Wall

Approach trail from Bruce's Parking Area

The Climbs

Routes are described right to left as they are encountered.

1. 1,000 Churches 10d ★
Seams and edges. 4 bolts, 40 feet

2. Ambro-Agie 12a ★★
Arête with 4 bolts. 35 feet

3. Obscured by Clowns 11b ★★
Beautiful smooth face with great edges. 5 bolts, 40 feet

4. Slick Fifty 12a ★
Arête on slick red rock. 5 bolts, 45 feet

5. Ziggurat 11d ★★
Dihedral on slick rock to ledges. 4 bolts, 45 feet

6. The Rift 12b ★★
Shallow corner on red wall to ledges above. 5 bolts, 45 feet

7. Bluebeard 11d ★★★
White corner with roof to steep juggy climbing above. 5 bolts, 50 feet

8. Mr. Big Shot 11a ★★
Steep wall with seam. 6 bolts, 50 feet

9. TS Headwall Arête. Open project.
This is the last local project Todd worked on before his death.

10. Project.

11. The Fun House 11c ★★
Starts on ledge at one-third height, up to summit. 100 feet

12. Soft Option 9 ★
Up easy corner to ledge, then up corner. 3 bolts, 40 feet

13. Kid Gloves 11c ★★
Up hard face past small ledge to fun steep moves. 4 bolts, 40 feet

14. Broken Heroes 13a ★
Small corner to bulge, then up smooth face above. 5 bolts, 40 feet

15. Big Smoke 11c ★★
Liebacks and jugs lead to a hard exit move. 4 bolts, 40 feet

16. Get Wacky 12b ★
Seam climb on black streak. 4 bolts, 40 feet

17. Bad Brain 13d ★★
Hard bouldery moves with the famous undercling crimp. 4 bolts, 45 feet

18. Full Tilt 13b ★★
Follows seam to hard top moves. 5 bolts, 40 feet

19. Project.

SPORT CLIMBS

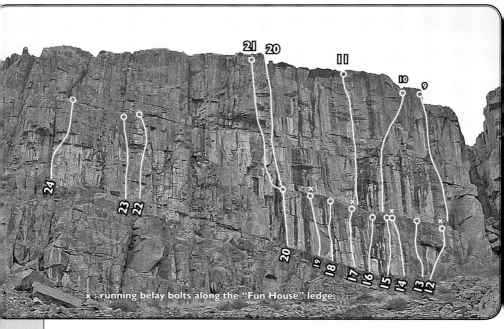

x : running belay bolts along the "Fun House" ledge.

20. Kilodeer 10a

Up groove past 4 bolts to anchor at ledge - 40 feet. The corner above is 5.11 and is protected with small cams and wires.

21. October Sky 13a ★

Start as for *Kilodeer*, moving left and up prow after low anchor. Tricky. 100 feet

22. I'm Ron Burgundy? 12a ★

Up deceptively overhanging wall on large holds to turn small roof on the right. 8 bolts, 55 feet

23. Twelfth Labor 11c ★

Corner with seam to steep headwall. 55 feet

24. Oral History 12a ★

Start up difficult arête, then turn a tricky roof before hitting the easy climbing. 6 bolts, 50 feet

LANDER S

FOSSIL HILL

This wonderful crag sits on the high ridge south of Sinks Canyon (see photos on page 15 & 140-141). Fossil Hill is bighorn dolomite, but tends to have more edges than pockets. It also tends to be a little taller than most of the local cliffs. This cliff sits at a higher elevation than the Sinks, and is slightly cooler in the summer.

The first climbs at Fossil Hill were done in the summer of 1991 by Frank Dusl and friends. The first season here yielded over half the routes at the cliff. Over the following years, the "usual suspects" Greg Collins, Todd Skinner, Dave Doll, Steve Bechtel, and Paul Piana added to this wonderful crag. Now boasting more than 50 climbs, this is a nice respite from the heat of Sinks Canyon and the endless pocket-pulling of Wild Iris.

DRIVE TIME: 20 minutes from Lander

HIKE: 15 minutes uphill

SUN EXPOSURE: Sunny 11 a.m. to 5 p.m.

SEASON: Spring, Summer and Fall; access limited in Winter

LENGTH: 50 to 100 feet

FOSSIL HILL ROUTE COUNT by GRADE

5.10 : 6 — **5.11** : 12 — **5.12** : 20 — **5.13** : 6 — **5.14** : 1

GETTING THERE (Fossil Hill)

The switchbacks leading to Fossil Hill, above Bruce's Parking Area, are usually closed from mid-November until the end of May. Drive up Sinks Canyon past the Bruce's Parking Area (11.3 miles from downtown), and up the switchbacks until the first hill is crested (about 5 miles past Bruce's). At this point, the cliff will be visible to your left, and a left turn possible on a small dirt road. Pull off on this road, and park in the small worn area below the 4WD scars on the hillside. See photo on next page.

As of Spring 2007, the Fossil Hill Road is being paved and road closures may vary. Check at Wild Iris Mountain Sports for the latest updates.

APPROACH (Fossil Hill)

The climbers' trail heads east of the ATV scars, and is a faint footpath heading at an easy diagonal incline. Follow this trail past a barbed-wire fence, and eventually into forest below the cliff. **The trail hits the cliff at route 34.**

Routes 1 and 2 might be best accessed by walking straight uphill from the parking area, as they are quite removed from the bulk of the climbs.

Routes 1 & 2

Climbers' trail to the Main Cliff and the rest of the climbs

Routes are described left to right across the cliff; although the trail hits the cliff at route 34.

1. The Swiss Indirect 11b
This route is at the prow of Fossil Hill, about 1/4 mile west of the main climbing.

2. The Dutch Directissimo 10c
Another route at the prow, no info.

3. Milk Bone 13a ★
Follows hard pockets up pretty orange wall 150 yards left of *Fossil Logic*. No photo. 5 bolts, 45 feet

FOSSIL HILL

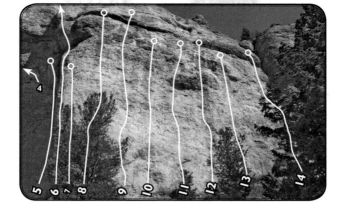

4. Project.
The high bulge, anchors only.

5. Fossil Logic 11c ★★
Start climbing up big corner, then move right and out big wave wall on big holds. 70 feet

6. Hell Bent for the Horizon 12d ★★
Up pretty and steep west facing wall. 110 feet

7. Project. Sound of Silence
The prow project.

8. Tremors 13a ★★
Hard long moves on crimps and monos. 70 feet

9. Unforgiven 12d ★
Continuously bouldery moves on some really thin holds. 70 feet

10. Channel Zero 11c ★★★
Enjoyable long moves up pretty streak. 65 feet

11. Household Chemicals 12b
Hard start to beautiful upper wall. 70 feet

12. Graboids 12a ★
Powerful moves low to fun bulge above. 70 feet

13. No Seats in Hell 11c ★★
Continuous climbing to a baffling crux. 70 feet

14. Furniture in Heaven 10a
Strange and filthy climbing. 60 feet

SPORT CLIMBS

Routes
4 to 14

Routes
15 to 24

Routes
25 to 31

Approach Trail

FOSSIL HILL

15. Highjackers 12c
Climb up seams and liebacks to hard moves. 60 feet

16. From Hell to Breakfast 12b
A pretty wall with hard long moves. 60 feet

17. Diamond Mouth 12c
Baffling crux after crux. Good climbing. 60 feet

18. Show Love 10d
Start in corner then go right and up face above. 65 feet

19. Project.

Routes
32 to 43

Routes
44 to 48

Routes
50 to 52

20. King of Fools 12b ★
Long and hard moves, crimps to high bulge. 80 feet

21. Queen of Spades 11d ★★
Crimpy start. Thin moves up vertical wall, then strenuous above roof to anchors. 80 feet

22. Project.
Face behind tree

23. The Empty Quarter 11d
Starts up thin flake to good moves. A bit burly through the bulge. 85 feet

24. The Full Nickel 11b ★
Good climbing on varied rock. 85 feet

25. Merely Mortal 11a ★★
Begin in corner, then up vertical wall to anchors. 80 feet

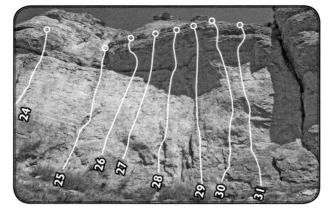

26. Vision of a Kiss 12b ★★
Fight through long moves on vertical rock to a really good bulge. 80 feet

27. Hips Like Cinderella 12c ★★★
One of the best. Hard low crux, then hard through high roof. 85 feet

28. The Saucy and the Brave 12c
Hard and weird low, great bulge high. 80 feet

29. Casual Entertainment 11c ★★★
Starts up big pillar, then up prow through bulges. 80 feet

30. Hang Fire 12a ★★★
Sustained difficulty and pump. Look for big hueco near bolt three. 80 feet

31.Tender Prey 12a ★★
Underclings and sidepulls lead to easier climbing above, then through tricky roof. 80 feet

32. Space Needle 12a ★★
Up crack in corner past tiny tree, then through two bulges. 70 feet

33. Two Ducks and an Angel 10b ★
Fun prow/corner route. 80 feet

34. Monster Match 13c ★★
Climb concave bulge to easy face above. 75 feet

35. Flying Roundhouse 12d ★★
Face to crack through bulge, then up headwall above. 11 bolts, 80 feet

36. Project.
7 bolts, 60 feet

37. The Ol' Double Diamond 12b ★
Crack in corner, then traverse right and up prow. 70 feet

38. The Legend of Norm 12b ★★
Start same as *Double Diamond*, but traverse right around prow to good, long moves up steep wall. 70 feet

39. When the Cubans Hit the Floor 14a ★★
Up crack/corner to rail through roof, then up hard wall above. 60 feet

40. Project.
Fibonacci Shimmer

41. The Righteous and The Wicked 13a ★★★
Underclings and crimps lead to easier climbing above. 90 feet

42. Unnamed 13b
Hard long moves.

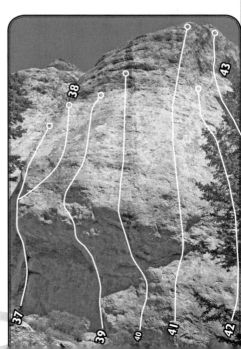

43. Fly Bones 13a ★
Just left of big corner up hard moves between good rests. 80 feet

44. Asian Rut aka Asian Orange 13c ★★
Beautiful orange streak on low-angle wall. 75 feet

45. Big in Japan 12a ★
Eleven bolts up face, then through prow. 80 feet

46. Maybe in the Next World 12a ★
Thin moves up slab, then through strenuous bulge. 80 feet

47. There Goes My Gun 11c ★★
Up seam then through cruxy bulge. 5.9 to first anchor. 75 feet

48. Vortec 10d
Hard slab to hard bulge. 65 feet

The trail drops away from the cliff near the route *Vortec*, working its way below the huge jumble of boulders.

49. Boom Stick 12a ★★

Short route on steep east wall of boulder near trail. No photo. 30 feet

50. Hero or Zero 11c ★★

Sustained difficulty to pumpy high crux. 80 feet

51. A Bullet for Mr. Ducky 10c ★★★

Great climbing up to water groove. 75 feet

52. Don't Call Me Shorty 11d ★

Shorter than the other routes on this wall, but thin. 50 feet

Canadian hardman, Scott Milton working *Orange for Anguish* (14+): "Orange" for the beautiful stone, "Anguish" for the 10+ year effort. Photo © Bobby Model. www.m-11.com

LANDER S

BALDWIN CREEK

Baldwin Creek's main cliff is one of the most beautiful in America. The stone is very compact and features mostly pocket climbing on slightly overhanging walls. The climbs range in the 50 to 90 foot range, and most are equipped with clip anchors. This cliff was primarily developed during the 1993-1994 climbing seasons, with a small crew of dedicated climbers establishing some of the best routes in the entire Lander area.

DRIVE TIME: 45 minutes from Lander

HIKE: 30 minutes flat and downhill
You approach via the top of the crag

SUN EXPOSURE: Sunny until 7 p.m. most of the year

SEASON: Cool Summer evenings and Fall

LENGTH: 60 to 90 feet

BALDWIN ROUTE COUNT by GRADE

5.10 :   2   —   **5.11** :   7   —   **5.12** :   26   —   **5.13** :   13

GETTING THERE (Baldwin Creek)

From downtown Lander head west on Main toward the mountains. Just after 9th street, Main veers right, heading north to a traffic light. Take a left here, on Baldwin Creek Road. Continue west on Baldwin Creek Road. Follow this paved road for 5.5 miles, until the road turns to the south (left) and it is possible to continue west on an improved dirt road. After 0.9 miles, the road splits, with the left fork heading into a ranch and the right fork (Shoshone Lake Road) taking you north along a big red butte. Follow this road up several switchbacks to the crest of a small hill (about 5 miles).

At the top of this hill is a parking area popular with ATV riders. From here on up, the road continues up through meadows and aspens and is very rough in spots and requires a high-clearance vehicle.

After 10 to 15 minutes of slow going, near the crest of a hill, you'll pass a cattle guard and an "Entering Public Lands" sign. About 100 yards later, there is a clear area to park on the left, just before the road heads back downhill into a wooded drainage. This is the Baldwin Creek climbing area trailhead. 13.5 miles from Main Street in Lander. Subaru Outbacks can make it but the extra clearance of a truck is better.

SPORT CLIMBS

APPROACH (Baldwin Creek)

From the parking area, walk west up the road for about 200 feet. There is a faint trail heading left (south) from here, and past a BLM trail kiosk that is 150 feet from the road. Follow a mostly flat path through a forest and over a small fence to an open meadow at the crest of a hill. This is a 12 to 15 minute walk so far.

Drop down the hill and follow faint switchbacks through a break in the cliff. Heading left as you go down the gully, you will find a footpath at the base of the cliff, taking you down the cliff, back to the east. See photo on page 159.

The first climbs you reach break through the long, high horizontal roof, about 200 yards along the cliff from the descent gully. The bulk of the climbs, however, are another 3 to 5 minutes along. Look for the slightly overhanging black wall of *Brave Cowboy*, and the lone "shade tree" near *Amused to Death*.

The Climbs

Routes described from left to right as they are encountered.

1. Skyliner 13b ★★
11c to first anchor at top of flake. Break the huge roof above left of a seam. 100 feet

2. Project.
Through roof right of *Skyliner*.

3. Magpies on an Afterbirth 12a
Gold shuts on slab, diagonals right. 75 feet

4. Project.
Right of gold shuts, direct line to end of *Magpies*.

5. Greased Lightning 12b
Starts below large bulge, climbs through bulge, then slightly left and up slab. 75 feet

6. Space Brigade 12b ★★
Up undercuts to steep wall. 95 feet

7. Swiss Miss 5.13a ★★
Less-than-vertical wall to anchors below square-cut roof. 90 feet

BALDWIN CREEK

BALDWIN & SUICIDE CLOSURES

The road to Baldwin is typically closed from mid-November to June 1 of each year. Additionally, there are occasional raptor nesting closures that last until July 15 of each year. Please contact Wild Iris Mountain Sports in Lander at (307) 332-4541 about any current or potential closures.

8. White Lightning 10d ★★
Starts in crack, then up right into left-facing dihedral. 80 feet

9. Daybreaker 13b
Hard start leads to tricky climbing on rounded prow. 65 feet

10 . Troubleshooter 13a ★★
Steep face, shares anchors with *Mask*. 45 feet

11. Mask Without a Face 12a ★★★
Up steep climbing on good holds through bulge. 45 feet

PORT CLIMBS

12. Hair Trigger 12b
Start on underclings and sidepulls; then through roof on difficult moves. 70 feet

13. Where There's A Will, There's A Way 12c
Up through black roof, very bouldery. 70 feet

14. Pizza Hut Girl 12b ★★★
Up small arête, then right along lip of big roof. After rightward traverse; up on pumpy moves to anchor. 75 feet

15. Sideshow Bob 13c ★
Short, boulder-problem route right of the *Pizza Hut* roof. 40 feet

16. Beelzebubba 12a ★
Climb up tricky right-facing corner to easier ground. 65 feet

17. Break Like The Wind 11d ★
Climb seam to vertical face above. 65 feet

18. I Am A Fat Man 12c ★
Bulging wall. 65 feet

19. Black Jacques Serac 13a
Hard moves through bulge, easier up high. 70 feet

LANDERS

Tricia Stetson climbing *Brave Cowboy* (12a).
Photo © Bobby Model. www.m-11.com

20. Lucky Thirteen 12d
Tricky seam climbing to pumpy wall above. Technical. 80 feet

21. Mephisto 12c ★★
Long moves on generally good pockets. 80 feet

22. Western Family 12d
Another tricky seam climb. 75 feet

23. Surfer Rosa 12c ★
Climb up a pretty gold wall to high bulge. 80 feet

24. Little Pedro's Mexican Tidal Wave 12b ★★
Hard low move then left to pumpy headwall. 80 feet

25. Barbarossa 12b ★
Shares start with *Little Pedro*; then up right to hard steep climbing. 80 feet

26. Brave Cowboy 12a ★★★
Excellent route; starts in shallow left-facing corner, then climbs through hard steep wave. 80 feet

27. Très Amigos 12c ★★★
Hard low moves lead to a good rest, then a continuous hard headwall. 75 feet

28. Viva Hate 13d ★★
Through steep moves to easier climbing at top. 75 feet

29. The Power of One 13a ★★
Hard mono moves lead to a gold streak. 80 feet

30. Project. No Cross, No Crown

31. Last Chance for a Slow Dance 12d ★
Climb up through steep wave, then right and up technical face above. 75 feet

32. Project.
Straight up into *Last Chance* finish.

33. Project.
Black streak. Steep and continuous.

BALDWIN CREEK

LANDERS

34. Graffiti Man 12c ★★
Starts on small prow; then up through small roofs along crack. 60 feet

35. Bittersweet 13c ★★
Very hard slab then through center of roofs. 70 feet

36. Supple Cowboy 13a ★
Climb left-facing corner to right side of roof; then up hard moves above. 60 feet

37. Project. Cowboy This

38. Project. Wishing Well

39. Access Denied 13a ★★
Monos and long moves lead through a black wall. 65 feet

40. Project. Follows black hangers.

41. State of Grace 12d ★
Very powerful moves up underclings and small pockets. 55 feet

42. Two Guys Names Festus 12d ★★★
Climb up long moves and thin pockets just left of the big tree. 65 feet

43. Amused to Death 12a ★★

Right of the big tree; climb up through left side of arch roof to spicy, yet easier, slab above. 70 feet

44. The Bravery of Being Out of Range 13a ★★

Climbs face to biggest part of roof; then up easier face above. 80 feet

45. Piston Hurricane 12b ★★★

Up good face to roof; through roof on good moves. 80 feet

46. TKO 12b ★★

Up right side of arch; then through roof. 80 feet

47. Rapid Fire 12b ★

Climb face just right of arch; continuous. 75 feet

48. Losing Streak 12b ★★★

A hard, beautiful grey streak. 80 feet

49. Voodoo Chile 11c

Starts on flake; up hard moves to easier slab above. 70 feet

50. Gimmie Shelter 11b ★★

Starts just left of large bush, climb up to undercling, over it, and up a good wall. 60 feet

51. Withering Heights 11a ★

Hard start just right of bush. Good pockets. 70 feet

52. One Trick Pony 11a
Poor and dirty climbing on a pretty-looking wall. 70 feet

53. Dinosaur Rock 10c ★★
Starts on grassy slope; climb on big pockets past small bulges. 60 feet

54. Ticket To Ride 11c ★
Good climbing on vertical wall left of orange roof/wave. 60 feet

55. Sunshine Superman 11b ★
Vertical, technical climbing. 65 feet

56. Can't Always Get What You Want 11d ★
Prow to slab. 65 feet

57. Rain of Gold 13b ★★★
Climb up arête to steep face above. 75 feet

58. Project. Orange For Anguish
Up arête, then right and through center of steep wave. 85 feet

59. Project.
Right side of wave.

Todd Skinner on *Wind Drinker* (12b).
Photo © Bobby Model. www.m-11.com

LANDER S

SUICIDE POINT

Suicide is Lander's most alpine sport climbing area. This crag is the western-most end of the mighty Baldwin Creek Wall, but is provided as a separate chapter since it is approached from a different parking area and is some three miles west of the bulk of the Baldwin Creek climbs. The rock at Suicide is wind-weathered and is very angular. Many routes follow cracks, corners, and other distinct features. One of the 5.9s take natural gear so for this climb bring a few medium-sized cams. The rest are all bolted sport climbs on the most wild and beautiful crag around Lander.

See page 149 for more information on road closures (seasonal and for raptor nesting) affecting Suicide Point access.

DRIVE TIME: 50 minutes from Lander

HIKE: 5 minutes uphill

SUN EXPOSURE: Sunny 10 a.m. to dark

SEASON: Summer and Fall

LENGTH: 50 to 120 feet

SUICIDE POINT ROUTE COUNT by GRADE

5.9 : 2 — **5.10 :** 1 — **5.11 :** 3 — **5.12 :** 5 — **5.13 :** 2

The Climbs

A climbers' path leads up to the huge prow (*Wind Drinker*). All described climbs are within two minutes of this prow.
See the next page for approach details. Climbs are described left-to-right.

1. Hurricane Hannah 11b ★

Start up arête below *Wind Drinker* (the VERY obvious prow), then move left around corner to steep face. This climb was done by Amy and Todd Skinner the summer after their first daughter, Hannah, was born. 80 feet

2. Wind Drinker 12b ★★★

Up easy arête to anchor (5.6), then out "hatchet blade" prow. See photo on the Contents page. 70 feet

GETTING THERE (Suicide Point)

Follow the directions getting to the Baldwin Creek trailhead. From there, the road flattens out and then begins climbing once you reach the bottom of the drainage. Just over 1 mile past Baldwin's parking, you'll begin driving through open meadows and should be able to see the dramatic prow of Suicide Point on the ridge to your left. Turn left toward this cliff on an obvious two-track road, and drive up to a nice parking area on the ridge below the cliffs. A faint trail leads to the base of the climbs.

3. Suicide King 12c ★★★

Easy face climbing right of arête leads to long pulls up overhanging rock. 80 feet

4. Storm Chaser 11d ★

Starts in crack, then up steeper face above. Be careful to avoid climbing right to the *Weeping Wrist* anchors. 80 feet

5. Weeping Wrist 11b

Thin face through bulge to anchor in alcove. 65 feet

6. A Cry for Help 10c

Up slab to horizontal, then up short steep wall. Bolted by Dave Brinda way back in 1991 and then abandoned for the "more accessible" climbs of Baldwin Creek. 55 feet

7. Open Project (5.12?)

Jamie Axelrod put the bolts in and never came back.

8. Flowers for a Dead Man 13b

Up center of steep face. 60 feet

9. Painless 9 ★★

Climbs the steep offwidth corner. Fun. Lilygren had a great habit of rolling in and snagging the classics at every new crag. 60 feet

10. Nickel Winchester 12b ★★

Up edgy face, finishing below the roof. 60 feet

11. Apocalyptic Lapse Rate 9

Climbs the dihedral with natural and fixed protection. Bring cams to 2". 80 feet

See page 149 for more information on road closures (seasonal and for raptor nesting) affecting Suicide & Baldwin.

Suicide Point at upper left-hand skyline. Baldwin Creek on the right (approach trail marked). This commanding cliff extends another two miles off to the right

12. Golden Ulric 12c ★★

Starts in corner, then out steep wall and through bulging rock above. 100 feet

13. Silver Nimschkie 13b ★★

Underclings through bulge, then up through thin pockets. 80 feet

14. Stormbringer 12d ★★★

Up corner to anchor (5.9), then out 20 foot horizontal roof. 75 feet

Suicide Point Overview

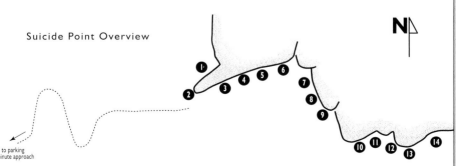

to parking
minute approach

159

PORT CLIMBS

FIRST ASCENTS by ROUTE

LANDERS

LANDERS

SPORT CLIMBS

LANDERS

ROUTE INDEX by GRADE

PORT CLIMBS

5.11a

5.11b

SPORT CLIMBS

ROUTE INDEX by GRADE

LANDERS

SPORT CLIMBS

LANDERS

CORRECTIONS & UPDATES

Please help us out and send in any of the following: errors or typos you find in this book; broken holds; to call bullshit on a sandbag; find a route line in the wrong place: or anything else you think might be useful. If you have established a new route, it is highly encouraged to let us know. This is not a canned plea for help. In reality, unsolicited updates are about as common as a Democrat winning a Wyoming Presidental election.

This makes it very time consuming and difficult to stay on top with accurate and updated information. The information that is most useful typically comes from the average yet passionate climbers that are out there weekend after weekend, hanging at the base and around the campfire with other core climbers, epicing on some obscure testpiece, or simply doing an easy standard for their umpteenth time.

Most people assume someone else has already reported the mistakes or submitted updates on a new line of bolts that appeared since last fall. It just ain't so. So *PLEASE*, no matter how random or insignificant any piece of information or photo may seem, every single bit helps. If there is something about this book you don't like, this is your chance to help us improve. An easy way to recieve a free copy of the next updated and expanded edition is if we publish your killer action shot (min 300 dpi or 35 mm film only). Future editions will be so much better for it and if nothing else, it will improve our ability to get them completed and available that much quicker. Thanks in advance.

Please send to:

PRESS

or

elemental
climbing

First Ascent Press
PO Box 2388
Livingston, MT 59047
or email to:
beta@firstascentpress.com

Elemental Training Center
134 Lincoln
Lander, WY 8250
or email to:
steve@elementaltraining.com

LOWER OFF A WORN OUT ANCHOR?
FIND A BOLT THAT NEEDS REPLACING?

Contact the author (at the above Lander address) or the staff at Wild Iris Mountain Sports. Wild Iris and local climbers do, from time to time, have money, equipment and manpower available to support the replacement of bolts and anchors.

See page 4 for more details.

Cowboy Rock

Series of Wyoming Climbing Guides

Upcoming Volumes of Cowboy Rock

Big Horn Rock Climbs
by Trevor Bowman

Do you love the bighorn dolomite climbing of Wild Iris and Ten Sleep; but feel intimidated because you aren't a 5.12 climber? If so, the crags on the east side of the Big Horn Mountains are your next climbing destination; featuring over 200 routes 5.11 and under on Wyoming's most popular sport climbing stone. Bonus beta includes the world-class alpine granite of the Cloud Peak Wilderness.

Wind River Rock Climbs
Cirque of the Towers & Deep Lake
by Steve Bechtel
Available Christmas 2007

Finally! A modern guide to the best alpine rock climbing in America. Written by one of the leading Wyoming pioneers, this guide features all the cirque peaks including Pingora, Wolf's Head, and Warbonnet; plus the Deep Lake area with Temple Peak and Haystack. This select guide will inspire a generation.

Volume 2 in the First Ascent High Point Map Series

Gannett Peak, 13,804 ft
A Topo Map and Climbing Guide to Wyoming's Highest Peak

The first All-in-One map and guide for one of the premier peaks in North America. Written by Tom Turiano and features a 1:63,500 map showing three major approaches; PLUS a new and unique 1:25,000 shaded topographic map centered on Gannett Peak. For the first time on a single map, you will find all the popular approaches, logistics, in-depth climbing descriptions, "light and fast" ascent stategies and aerial photos with route lines for the Wind River Range's most popular summit.

PRESS

First Ascent Press

Livingston, Montana